Gardening
SOS

To Michael, Rowan and Meg

Gardening

SOS

Your problems solved

LIA LEENDERTZ

guardianbooks

2 4 6 8 10 9 7 5 3 1

Copyright © Lia Leendertz 2010

Lia Leendertz has asserted her right under the Copyright, Designs
and Patents Act, 1988, to be identified as the author of this work

First published in Great Britain in 2010 by
Guardian Books
Kings Place, 90 York Way
London N1 9GU

www.guardianbooks.co.uk

A CIP catalogue record for this book
is available from the British Library

ISBN 978-0-85265-206-0

Designed and typeset by www.carrstudio.co.uk
Printed and bound in Great Britain by Clays Ltd, St Ives PLC

Contents

Acknowledgments

I would like to thank everyone I have worked with at the *Guardian*, and in particular Susie Steiner and Jane Perrone. Susie took a chance on me in the first place, asking me to become the *Guardian*'s gardening correspondent, and Jane has been a hugely inspiring and supportive gardening editor.

The knowledge contained within these pages is not all mine. I have frequently had to call upon nursery owners, experts and gardeners for their specialist expertise. Where they have helped me, I have mentioned them, but I would like to acknowledge their help here, too. I would also like to thank Leigh Hunt and Guy Barter of the RHS advisory service, who have kept me straight with the most up-to-date information on many occasions.

The column and this book would not exist without its readers and correspondents. I am often asked if I make the questions up – apparently this is fairly common in gardening Q&As – but the honest truth is I have never had to because there have always been so many.

Thanks to all those who have ever written in, and keep the letters coming. Finally, I would like to extend my thanks to Katherine Le Ruez for her careful selection and meticulous editing.

Introduction

Doctors often complain that they are never off duty; friends surreptitiously flash them unusual rashes at dinner parties, and neighbours cobble them in the supermarket about their impacted haemorrhoids. The life of a gardening Q&A writer is not all that dissimilar. In the five years since I became the *Guardian*'s gardening agony aunt I have been asked about stubborn ivy tendrils while on the school run, and the best plants for a shady, dry spot while swimming lengths. Almost every time I visit any relative I am taken on a mini tour entitled 'the pests, diseases and dying bits of my garden'.

To say it doesn't bother me is an understatement. It delights me. It fills me up with pride. Everyone wants to believe their job is worthwhile, and being frequently pestered for answers to gardening conundrums proves to me that mine is. People want to know about gardening. It is often made out to be a tricky business: very technical, with complicated Latin names, and lots to learn before you can carry it out successfully. But in fact it's really not, and a little nudge in the right direction is often all a gardener needs to feel more confident in their abilities.

It is the little nudge that I try to provide, but I have noticed, reading back over these entries, that the direction of my nudges has changed slightly over the years. This is partly down to my own evolution as a gardener, and partly down to *Guardian* readers. It is hard to write into a vacuum, with no feedback, and no idea of where you are going right or wrong, or even if anyone is reading you. This has never been an issue with these columns. The very nature of a Q&A column encourages communication between reader and writer, and *Guardian* readers are an intelligent and vocal bunch. Feedback has often been swift and sometimes harsh.

The most notable examples were regarding garden chemicals. I have always gardened more or less organically, but when I started writing these columns I included information about garden chemicals, believing it was what people wanted to know. I soon noticed that I got a flurry of complaints every time a pesticide or herbicide was mentioned, and started to question my wisdom on the matter, and indeed my own gardening. Slowly my position hardened, I became more militant in my own garden, and I now look for organic alternatives wherever possible. I am not sure if it was a process I would have gone through anyway – it has been a time of change in the world of gardening – or if I have simply been influenced by a desire to get fewer complaint letters, but I do think I am a better gardener for having listened to my readers. I hope a few of them feel the same way about me.

In this book you will find a collection of the questions I have been sent over the last five years and the answers I have given, although I have taken the liberty of tweaking a few of the answers where I felt they were really out of step with the answers I would give were I sent the same question today. There are also a few ideas each week for jobs you might do in your garden. I hope you find the answers to your worries within, and that this book gives you just the nudge you need to get out and enjoy your garden.

Lia Leendertz, March 2010

Spring

A spring garden can be a flurry of blossom and bulbs, or it can be a muddy rugby pitch with some bare earth and sticks around the edges. If your garden is lacking interest in spring, you can't remedy it entirely at the time, but you should set your alarm for next autumn, when you can plant bulbs, and next winter, when you can plant bare-root trees. In fact, container grown trees and shrubs for blossom can still be planted in spring, but they won't have time to get established before summer, so you will need to remember to water them well all year. Spring flowering perennials such as pulmonaria, dicentra, and primula associate beautifully with bulbs, and these can be bought and planted now, while they're in flower and you can really see what you're getting.

A common pitfall at this time of year is failing to protect plants from late frosts, and it's important to keep watching the forecasts if you have fruit trees or tender plants. Keep tender plants such as dahlias safely tucked away until you are pretty sure all frosts have passed, and when you do plant them out be ready and prepared to step in and protect them should a cold snap strike. Keep some horticultural fleece to hand to throw over them and fruiting trees – if they get hit when the blossoms are out, you will lose your entire crop for the year. Fruit trees such as apricots and peaches may also struggle for pollinators, as they blossom so early in the year that there aren't many around. Take a soft paintbrush and tickle each blossom to help things along.

Later in spring, as strawberries start to grow and flower, you should mulch underneath them with straw to lift the flowers and fruit away from the mud. This prevents rotting and also makes them less easy prey for slugs, which love strawberries just as much as we do.

Lawns start growing in spring, and you will need to start mowing. If you have an adjustable mower, make the first cut fairly high, lowering it gradually over the following few weeks. You can also still mend straggly lawns, by laying new turf or overseeding patchy bits.

I get a great many queries later in the year about plants that fail to flower, but this is actually the time to act to put things right. There are all sorts of reasons why a plant may not flower, but it is always worth giving a couple of feeds with a high potash fertiliser to remind them what they're meant to do. Roses will really appreciate this and give you a great show later.

Spring is the time to start vegetable seedlings off, but problems often occur if you sow too early or too late. In early spring sow broad beans, spinach, broccoli, leeks, rocket, cabbages, and peas. Potatoes can be planted out too. Gardeners are always keen to get their tender vegetables – the glamour crops – up and running, but sow too early and you will have to keep them indoors for too long, and they won't fare well when they do finally get out into the garden. In terms of harvesting, this can be a bit of a lean time, but if you've planned ahead you may have purple-spouting broccoli, leeks, rhubarb, spring onions, spring cabbage and asparagus. Also on the allotment, you need to be digging earth over and clearing the ground of weeds ready for an influx of plants.

Spring is the time when the gardener's nemesis – the slug – can do its worst damage. Slugs and snails love tender, young growth, and they can wipe out all of your carefully nurtured young plants overnight. Guard against them carefully.

Beginning of March

We're buying a new-build property with a blank garden and would like to plant some fast-growing trees for privacy. We had willow, conifers, cherry and apple at our last home, but suspect we will be long gone before new specimens reach maturity. Any suggestions?

You need to make sure they are not going to become so big as to become a pain in the future, so avoid notorious fast-growers such as willow, eucalyptus and poplar. Although these would provide the privacy you're after, they just don't know when to stop growing. Robinia, on the other hand, is an airy tree that is a quick grower, while rowans are fast-growing but stay compact, and birches are also rapid growers, but not overbearing. And you really must plant a paulownia, otherwise known as the foxglove tree – it is vigorous, will reach a satisfyingly tree-like stature within just a few years, and is also manageable. What's more, its big, felty leaves will become larger the more the tree is cut back.

I have bought some water butts, and read somewhere that charcoal in the water helps keep it 'sweet'. How do I set this up and how long does it last?

Charcoal is not particularly effective at stopping the water in butts from getting smelly. The best preventative is to stop debris from getting washed in via the downpipe from the gutter that feeds it. Fit a filter made of close chicken wire to the bottom of the pipe, and clean it out regularly. Siting the butts in a fairly cool and shaded spot will also help. That said, plants are not as fussy as we are when it comes to water, and don't care whether or not it smells, so you can splash it around freely, even without a filter. It's best to avoid using such water on seedlings, however, because it can carry a fungus that causes 'damping off', leading to patches of seedlings rotting at the base and collapsing.

Ground ivy is starting to grow into the lawn. Will it take over?

Ground ivy (Glechoma hederacea) is a weed of damp and shady places, and on damp and shady lawns is likely to out-compete the grass, which is weakened by such conditions. Try improving lawn drainage by pushing a garden fork into the ground at intervals of a foot or so, and brushing a mixture of sand and topsoil into the holes. If you can let in more light by pruning, this will help the grass to compete. Lawn weedkillers go only for broad-leaved plants such as this, so could work: apply when the ivy is in active growth. Finally, you could try to live with it. It is more closely related to thyme, sage, mint and marjoram than to ivy, and has pretty violet flowers and a minty, herby scent when mown.

Four years ago, we planted an Acer saccharum in our small garden in damp but well-composted soil. It got powdery mildew two years ago, so we sprayed it with a fungicide. This worked at first but then new leaves acquired the mildew and curled at the edges. Should we keep spraying?

So much chemical use could be avoided with good plant selection. Your garden centre sold you the wrong tree, and no amount of sprays will change that. Acer saccharum is the Canadian sugar maple and grows to at least 65ft in height with a 40ft spread. Surprised? It is a park or large garden tree and grows magnificently if given the space and air to stretch out into the landscape. It will fade away in a small urban garden as it is incredibly sensitive to cramped, close conditions and compacted soil – the powdery mildew and leaf scorch are signs of how stressed it is. While it is always horrid to get rid of a tree, this one is set to become a manky, diseased burden. Better to replace it. A Japanese maple would love your sheltered and moist setting. These are great small garden trees, with fabulous autumn colour, and many of them reach an eventual size of just 15ft. Check out Acer palmatum 'Linearilobum' (15ft high, deeply cut foliage), 'Bloodgood' (15ft, dark red leaves turning bright red in autumn) or 'Sango-kaku' (20ft, yellow leaves and bright red stems). If even these sound too big, there are smaller ones. Incorporate lots of grit and compost into your planting hole: although they need moisture, they must also have good drainage.

Is it possible (or advisable) to grow potatoes in a plastic dustbin?
Big containers suit potatoes well, although yields are lower than in the ground. Water is the big issue: too little, and you get measly results; too much, and tubers rot. Your goal is an even moistness. First earlies are best – an RHS trial has tipped 'Mimi' as top for container growing. A bin is a bit deep, though, because the sides cut out light from the plants, so after drilling drainage holes build up the base with crocks and compost to about 30cm. Put in two or three seed potatoes and cover with compost. As they grow, earth up by adding more compost to cover the stems. This keeps frost and light away from the tubers and encourages productive roots. Chit now (put in a cool, bright place to sprout) and plant at the end of March.

I have four Phyllostachys aurea that I would like to 'tame' to grow sideways, as a hedge. I believe a planting trench is the solution, but how deep and wide should it be, and what should I use to line it?
Golden bamboo (P. aurea) shoots out only the occasional runner, so may not warrant the huge digging job you're about to take on. However, a trench is the best way to keep the clump a definite 'hedge' shape. Angle the sides of the trench outwards, so shoots grow up and out, rather than down and under, and make it at least 60cm deep. Paving slabs and corrugated iron make good barriers (pond liner is rubbish: shoots pierce straight through it), or try bamboo root barrier (from bigplantnursery.co.uk), made from laminated, triple-woven nylon. Line the sides, but not the base, of the trench with the barrier. Leave it protruding 8cm above soil level. Make an annual check and chop off any shoots loitering near the boundary.

What to do this week

Aphids will soon be smothering the young, tender growth emerging from roses and fruit trees. Hopefully, later on, natural predators will kick in, but in the meantime young growth could become contorted, to say nothing of the effect on flowers and fruit. The solution? Both greenfly and blackfly hate soap, which clogs them up, preventing breathing. You can mist with washing-up liquid and water, or you can simply pour cooled washing-up water straight over your roses. If this is done every day, the aphids won't stand a chance.

Clematis that flower in late summer should get the chop now. Cut young plants back hard, to a pair of buds within 30cm of the ground, to encourage a bushy habit with fewer bare stems. Older plants can be pruned by about half (to stop them from flowering at the tops only) and have tangled stems removed. Don't forget to feed and water after pruning.

This is the moment to prune and feed blueberry plants. Don't bother if they are less than three years old (but don't expect much from such young ones, either). On older plants, remove any little whippy growths right to the base – they are a bad lot and will never amount to anything. Likewise, take out the dead and the manky. Shorten long growths to encourage the fruiting side branches to break from lower down, and prune flowered shoots to a low, strong-growing shoot. Feed with an ericaceous fertiliser such as rhododendron and azalea feed.

Early to mid March

I want a rose hedge. My heart's set on a fragrant, almost thornless rose such as purple 'Cardinal de Richelieu', but I wonder if it would be happy in poor, stony soil. Need I go for a tough, thorny rugosa?

Over time, you can improve even the poorest soil. Incorporate well-rotted manure or compost before planting, and mulch annually. Also incorporate Rootgrow (from davidaustinroses.com), which contains mycorrhizal fungi that help plants get the most out of whatever soil they are in. Rose expert Michael Marriott says that 'Cardinal de Richelieu' is not the most fragrant. He suggests instead the soft pink 'Mortimer Sackler' and the yellow 'Buttercup' and 'Molineux' as toughies with good fragrance and few thorns. The gallicas – such as the raspberry-rippled Rosa gallica 'Versicolor', maroon-crimson 'Tuscany' or deep pink 'Empress Josephine' – have small bristles rather than thorns and are very tough and suckering, so make good hedges.

I have a six-month-old avocado tree which I grew from a stone. I water it once a week and let it dry out in-between. In the past month, almost all the leaf edges have turned dry and brown, and several have dropped.

Watering once a week sounds quite a lot over winter, when it will not have been actively growing. Lift the pot before watering to see how heavy it is, rather than checking if the surface is dry. It may not recover if its roots have rotted. Growing a new one should take only a few months. Clean a stone and let it dry overnight, then suspend it, pointy end up, in water, so the bottom third is submerged. You can use a hyacinth vase, or push three toothpicks into the seed horizontally to create a sort of tripod. Keep it out of direct light and roots should appear within a few months, followed by a shoot. Pot into very well drained compost, such as cactus compost, leaving just the shoot showing.

I have lots of vegetable seeds left over from when I had an allotment. Some are 10 years old. Is it safe to sow them and eat the crops?

The only danger is that you may not get good rates of germination. The success rate depends partly on how the seeds have been stored, and partly on which seeds they are. Ideally, all seeds should be stored somewhere cool, dark and dry, with little fluctuation in temperature – maybe in paper packets inside a plastic container, in a shed. According to vegetable guru Sue Stickland's book, *Back Garden Seed Saving* (eco-logicbooks.com), you can expect most seeds to last about three years if stored well. An exception is parsnip, which cannot be kept longer than one year. Cabbages, cauliflowers, sprouts and their ilk should keep for up to five years, as should tomatoes. Squash and pumpkin are among the longer-lived seeds – up to 10 years. You may get a few seedlings beyond these dates, but you will waste a lot of time and compost, and it is a false economy not simply to buy fresh.

Two years ago I planted 30 one-year-old asparagus crowns on a friend's allotment. I've just taken over a plot of my own and would like to move them. When and how should I do this?

Asparagus don't like being moved, resenting it more and more as they get older. Also, if you are going to move them, do it while they're dormant, which means before the spears start to emerge. If you still want to give it a go, do it soon. Prepare the soil in the new bed first (weed it, then feed it by digging in lots of well-rotted manure or garden compost), then dig up the crowns, taking as much soil as you can from around them, to avoid damaging those fleshy, grumpy roots. Transport them in buckets, or wrap them in plastic bags to keep the rootball intact. Resist picking the spears this year to give the plants a chance to recover (and forgive).

I've been advised to pull out an old, gnarly lilac tree as it's not doing a lot in the flowering department. However, I love its twisty trunk and general shape. Can I breathe new life into it with some hard pruning or is its time up?

There is always such a race to correct or rip out plants that aren't performing perfectly. If you like it, keep it. Lilacs can reach a grand old age, and such old timers may not flower as profusely as young 'uns, but they bring much else to the party. Apart from the shape you love, yours is providing privacy and imbuing maturity. Renovation involves chopping the plant right down to ground level (or taking out a third at a time, where possible). Your lilac will take this in its stride, but you'll be left with a broad, rounded, spreading bush. This is the shape lilacs are 'meant' to be, but is it what you want? Leave yours be, but coax out more flowers by increasing the alkalinity around its roots with a sprinkling of lime and a mulch of mushroom compost.

I have discovered rats in my plastic kitchen waste composter. I'm worried about using poison because I have three cats. What can I do?

The rats are after shelter, warmth and food, so make the bin less welcoming and they may go elsewhere. Lift off the whole structure to expose the contents to the elements – rats don't like wet, cold nests. If you're feeling brave, spread out the compost, too. The usual advice is to avoid adding scraps of meat, fish and anything cooked or easily edible, including fruit and bread, but that doesn't leave much. You could try a Bokashi bin (bokashibucket.co.uk), for which you use an inoculated bran to 'pickle' scraps pre-composting, making them a turn-off to rats. It's a bit of a faff and not cheap, but you won't have to put perfectly compostable stuff in the waste bin.

What to do this week

Windowsill propagators, your moment has arrived. Tender vegetable plants (tomatoes, courgettes, peppers, sweet corn, squash, cucumbers, aubergines basically, all the exciting stuff) sown now will be ready to plant out in about six weeks' time, coinciding with likely last frost dates (see gardenaction.co.uk/main/weather.asp to find yours). You will have compact, healthy little plants just ready to stretch their legs, unlike the leggy, stressed-out ones clogging up the windowsills of gardeners too quick off the starting block.

If you grow your hostas in pots to keep those pesky molluscs at bay, you need periodically to scrape off the top of the soil to expose any round, white slug eggs or babies before they get the chance to start nibbling. Pick them out and dispose of them, top up the pot with new soil, then buy one of those big pots of Vaseline and slick a 4cm band of the stuff around the top of the pot. Take care that no leaves are overhanging the edge of the pot, thereby allowing daredevil slugs a sneaky route in.

From now and for the next couple of months, birds will be making great use of your hedges for nesting, so it is far better to look messy than risk disturbance by trimming. There are other ways you can help successful breeding: provide some extra calcium in the form of washed, crumbled eggshells on bird tables and provide soft nesting material, such as short lengths of wool and human or animal hair, kept tidy in a net orange bag.

Mid March

I want an instant evergreen screen, about 6–9m high and 6m wide, for privacy and to shield a neighbour's untidy garden. I've thought of putting up a split bamboo screen with quick-growing climbers.

Are you trying to force me to recommend leylandii? Obviously you can't put up a screen 9m high – that's just silly – so I suppose the best option is to plant a row of fast-growing, evergreen hedging plants, and yes, asbo-baiting leylandii is by far the quickest growing. But you need to know that it reaches 27m unchecked, and even at 9m could block out all light and sap all nutrients from the soil. Would a smaller hedge not suffice? Some alternatives to consider are the slower growing Thuja plicata 'Atrovirens', beautiful but leisurely Taxus baccata (yew) or even golden leylandii, which grows to about 12m unpruned. If you must plant leylandii, buy a good hedge trimmer, cut it twice a year without fail, and don't tell anybody I told you to.

A neighbouring business has installed on its walls five very bright, dusk-to-dawn security lights. It has refused to shade or shield the lights from our garden, which is now lit up all night. What effect will this have on our plants, birds and wild animals?

Plants anticipate the seasons by counting night length, and a break in the night is likely to make some plants delay flowering. This will be most noticeable in late summer- and after autumn-flowering plants, which will wait and wait for nights to lengthen, may never flower, and may not then prepare for winter, leaving them vulnerable to frosts. Constant light can reset birds' biological clocks, even leading them to nest in autumn rather than spring, and night light is known to have an effect on frog reproduction. Go back and talk to them again, and if you get nowhere contact the environmental health department of your local authority, telling them you want to make a complaint about light trespass. They will visit to see the extent of the problem and, if they consider the light to be causing a nuisance, they will take action to force the company to adopt good practice.

I live in a high-rise with a balcony and have a few things in pots, but the wind seems to kill everything except the geraniums. Can you recommend some hardy, wind-resistant plants that will brighten up the place?

In such extremely windy conditions you need some bulletproof plants with thick, leathery leaves, which protect them from drying out and can take a bit of a battering without showing too much damage. This does mean you can use some dramatic-shaped plants such as phormiums, cordylines and yuccas, all of which have large, sword-shaped leaves. Also consider dwarf conifers such as Pinus mugo and the low, spreading junipers. Hebes will give windproof flowers to go with your geraniums. The ornamental grasses carex, stipa and calamagrostis will provide swaying movement. Use pots with vertical sides to get maximum stability with minimum weight.

We want to move two 5ft-high box plants. Does box like moving? We want to put them in sunken containers to restrict root growth, as they are to be planted near the house.

No established shrubs actually like moving, but while some absolutely won't tolerate it, box will. Your beauties should recover with the right treatment. Now is a good time to do it. Deciduous shrubs and trees want moving while the leaves are off over winter, but evergreens transplant best in autumn or spring, when there is some active growth. First, though, reconsider your sunken container idea. Moving these large plants into a pot, where they cannot put out roots to search for water and nutrients, will prevent them from ever re-establishing themselves: they will be as dependent as houseplants. Insurance companies like to make us worry about invasive plant roots, but box has surface roots and is certainly no bullish drain or foundation invader. Instead, dig large holes and put in a generous amount of garden compost or well-rotted farmyard manure, forking over the bottom to mix some with your soil. Then trim back each plant as much as possible without ruining its shape – water is lost via leaves, and this counters the inevitable reduction in water-absorbing roots. Dig a trench around the outside of each plant and then work your way under, taking as much root as possible. Slide some tarpaulin beneath. You'll need at least one helper to shift them. Once each is in its hole, backfill a little at a time with compost and soil, treading it down gently as you go. Then give each a couple of buckets of water: rain is insufficient for the newly transplanted. Mulch with bark chippings or compost, and water all summer long.

I'd like to grow cucumbers this year, but all previous attempts have resulted in short stumpy gherkin types that are very bitter. Can you please recommend some varieties? Do I need a greenhouse?

I have only ever grown one type of cucumber, having previously been put off by experiences such as yours. Last spring I spotted the range of cucumbers offered by Real Seeds realseeds.co.uk. They don't offer any greenhouse cucumbers as they believe these are difficult to grow and don't taste particularly good. Theirs can be grown in the greenhouse or outdoors. I tried 'Miniature White' and it was a resounding success: short, pale, sweet, crunchy cucumbers were produced all summer long on compact vines. It became an instant favourite and will be a regular in my garden.

Can you tell me which variety of potato has the best resistance to slugs?

There are a large number of varieties that are said to offer some (but not complete) resistance, but slugs show the least interest in 'Kestrel', a second early noted for making marvellous chips and roasties. Others worth trying are 'Pentland Squire', 'Romano',

'Nadine' and 'Ulster Chieftain'. 'Sante' is the organic grower's favourite, because of its high resistance to almost everything and its versatile nature in the kitchen. One of the best things you can do if you are blighted by slugs (that's everyone, then) is harvest your potatoes by late summer, or as they reach maturity. No one knows why, but the onset of slug damage coincides with the completion of tuber growth.

What to do this week

Sweet peas are usually sown in autumn to make good summer plants. If you didn't get around to it, and don't want to sow seeds now, buy ready-grown seedlings known as plugs. They're fantastic trained up obelisks or bamboo-cane wigwams, making towers of scent and colour.

Rocket will germinate at fairly low temperatures and can bolt when the weather turns warm. As such, it is the perfect crop for in-between times, such as now. Sow a small row in fine soil, then repeat every few weeks for a succession, keeping soil moist. From early summer, rocket becomes a martyr to flea beetles, which riddle it with unappetising-looking holes. Cover with fine netting, such as Enviromesh (from organiccatalogue.com), to keep them at bay.

As soon as your daffodil flowers have faded, snap them off to stop the plant putting its energy into setting seed, and give the leaves a weekly dose of liquid feed to help build up the bulbs. But the single most important factor in ensuring a good show next year is (now come on, you know this one) to leave those leaves alone. No tying in knots, absolutely no quick tidy-up with the shears. Yellowing and unsightly as they are, just let them be.

Late March

I have a 4ft white camellia that is covered in buds over the winter. As they grow, however, the squirrels arrive and devour them. I'm endlessly chasing them away, but they stand there, arrogant and fearless, chomping away until there is not a single flower left. What can be done?

You might find a battery of techniques holds the little devils at bay just long enough for you to enjoy your blooms. Although it rankles, try putting out a constant supply of some of their favourite treats, such as peanuts and raw corn on the cob. Also, paste peanut butter on to the limbs of the bush: they can't resist it, but it clogs up mouths and paws, and keeps them occupied with cleaning for several hours at a time. Fill up a load of bird feeders of different designs, purely to encourage the squirrels to try to break into them, and put out large nuts in their shells for them to cart off and bury. Finally, make your own squirrel repellent: put a handful of hot peppers into a large bowl and pour over boiling water. Leave overnight, strain off and add a few drops of washing-up liquid, then pour into a spray bottle. When the plant is not in direct sunlight, spray all over.

I have a standard bay in a large planter, which I repotted last summer. It has since produced two sticks with leaves in the compost, but not attached to the trunk. Can these be cultivated into new plants, and if so, how?

These growths are known as suckers, and they are shoots that arise from the roots, sometimes as the result of damage. They can be separated from the main plant and grown on. This is a quick way of propagating new plants, but it does hold risks for the mother plant. Early spring is the time to do it, just before the plant has started into active growth. You will need to cut around the sucker with a spade or trowel and take enough root to allow the new plant to survive, but at the same time try not to take so much that you harm the original. Between six and eight inches from the sucker would be perfect for it, but this is likely to be too much for the mother plant, so use your judgment. Fill the hole with compost. Pot the new plants into fresh compost and keep them well watered and in a shady spot over the summer. They can then be planted out or put into larger pots.

The branches on our tall, thin cypress have started falling open, destroying its shape. We have tried tying them up and cutting them off to no avail.

Some fastigiate trees (trees with almost vertical branches) just start doing this as they age. Have another go at tying up the whole tree, rather than just the offending branches. Start with a long, strong piece of twine, and tie it firmly to a good branch at the base. Then wind it round in a spiral up the whole length of the tree and tie it to the central stem somewhere not too near the top.

I'm looking for a flowering evergreen plant or climber to fill a container. The space faces south-east, so can get very hot in summer, and I live in Devon, so the climate is mild. I would particularly like something exotic.

I spoke to Graham Jeffery, owner of Trevena Cross Nurseries (trevenacross.co.uk) in Cornwall, which specialises in rare and exotic plants that will grow in the milder parts of Britain. For an unusual climber, he suggests Abutilon megapotamicum, which is often grown as a conservatory plant but should do well in your conditions. It reaches heights of around 2.5m and has bright red and yellow pendulous flowers in spring and summer. Jeffery says you could also get away with a citrus, and recommends the lemon cultivar 'Meyer', which keeps its glossy green leaves all winter and should produce fruit in a warm site. Two suggestions from the southern hemisphere would make really unusual specimens: callistemons, the Australian bottle-brushes, produce a short-lived but spectacular display of spiky flowers in summer, and the South African Leucadendron 'Safari Sunset', grown mainly for its winter display of beautiful red bracts (used by florists) which last from November to April.

I have near a fence a birch tree whose roots are pushing up my neighbours' garden path. I've been told that pruning roots is risky if they are close to the trunk, and I don't want to pull the tree down. What can I do?

Pruning roots at the trunk makes the tree unstable, and you risk it dying and even falling down in high winds. The main problem is the removal of the structural support provided by large roots, but the loss of smaller roots that provide water will further weaken the tree. Birch trees root across the soil surface, making them sensitive to such treatment. If your neighbours' path is at a fair distance from the tree, they might be able to cut the roots next to the path, but consult a qualified arborist before attempting this. Otherwise, tell them to move their path.

I'd like to fill a gap by a boundary with something spiky to prevent intruders. The hole is 3ft from a beech tree and 1ft down I hit large roots. Will anything grow here?

As long as you don't expect an instant burglar barricade, a mahonia may be in with a chance. You could also try the formidable Chinese holly, Ilex cornuta or the hedgehog holly, Ilex aquifolium 'Ferox Argentea', which is as pretty as it is bristly. Fill the hole with organic matter (mushroom or garden compost) and put in the smallest plant you can find (large ones will need more sustenance than this spot can give – a small one will send out exploratory roots and hopefully find a way to be self-sustaining). Water frequently to get it established.

What to do this week

It's time to get supports in place for emerging herbaceous plants. If it's done now, plants will grow through and quickly hide them but if you leave it until after they've flopped, they will look trussed up and awkward for the rest of the year. Twiggy prunings from shrubs and trees are perfect – or make your own with stakes pushed into the ground in a square and then strung with wire or with a chicken wire lid. On the other hand, just buy them – try Ferndale Lodge (ferndale-lodge.co.uk).

That scrap of yellowing lawn could be a glorious green sward by summer if you pamper it now. Scratch out dead bits of grass with a spring-tined rake, then mow lightly with the blades set high to take off the tips. If you don't have a grass box on your mower, gather up the loose scratchings. Loosen the surface of the soil with the rake before sowing a grass seed mix. Water in, using a seaweed-based feed, such as Maxicrop Ultra Lawn Fertiliser. To steal a march on hungry birds, pre-germinate the seed by soaking it in water for a week or so – you'll need to change the water frequently.

Seeds sown directly into the soil now will struggle in the damp and cold. So delay sowing of hardy annuals such as lettuce, carrots and beetroot for a couple of weeks, and cover their intended bed for the time being with a sheet of clear or black plastic. The sun will warm the soil beneath them more effectively than it would do without, readying it to welcome the seeds next month. As an added bonus, the extra heat will encourage weed seedlings to raise their heads, and these can then be hoed off before sowing, so cutting down on competition for your annuals.

End of March / beginning of April

Twelve years ago, I planted a winter-flowering evergreen clematis that should have produced small white flowers. In mid-February this year it flowered for the first time – not many, but much appreciated. Last year, I trimmed the plant at its edges. What should I do to ensure a repeat?

Winter-flowering evergreen types such as Clematis cirrhosa and its cultivars don't really need pruning, unless they start to get too untidy and out of hand, in which case they can have a little haircut just after flowering. They then have the rest of the year to put on and ripen up growth for the next winter's flowering. Ruth Gooch of Thorncroft Clematis Nursery (thorncroft.co.uk) thinks your problem might be down to a lack of feed. For any clematis not producing as many flowers as it should, she suggests watering a liquid tomato fertiliser (high in flower-promoting potassium) on to the roots once a fortnight, from May to September, or scattering and watering in a handful of sulphate of potash in early summer and early autumn.

I want some shrubs for winter interest in my small (4ft x 8ft), sunny front garden. Would dogwood be too large?

Only if left unpruned. Dogwoods can be cut back to within a few inches of the ground every spring. This keeps them compact and produces the best coloured winter stems. Daphne cneorum 'Eximia' is a ground-cover shrub with strong fragrance and pink flowers. Get round your space problem by training Abeliophyllum distichum or Lonicera fragrantissima against a wall. Both have scented winter flowers.

Mosquitoes are breeding in my water butt. What is the best method to stop them?

A tight-fitting lid helps, but often they sneak in anyway. Try a slick of olive oil. Mosquito larvae hang below the surface and oil prevents them from breathing. Olive oil is less likely than other oils to break up and contaminate the water, and it takes longer to go smelly – even so, you will still need to skim it off and replace it every few weeks. An alternative is to let a couple of goldfish loose in the butt. This is apparently effective (they gobble up the mosquitoes) but seems a little cruel to me – what sort of a life is that? If you have some goldfish in a pond or tank, you could perhaps pop them in for an occasional killing spree and return them home after they've done their worst.

I saw a lovely 'garden-on-a-wall' at the musée du quai Branly in Paris: grasses, mosses and ferns. Could I try this on my loose slate wall in my damp backyard in north Wales?

You have described Patrick Blanc's ingenious planting system, Le Mur Végétal (verticalgardenpatrickblanc.com). It uses metal frames to hold plants in place, which are watered and fed via drip irrigation (no soil). Blanc was inspired by plants growing in rock crevices, surviving on dripping water. The low-tech approach is to direct-sow small, spreading plants (such as Ajuga reptans, Campanula poscharskyana, Alchemilla alpina, Iberis sempervirens and Aquilegia jonesii all from chilternseeds.co.uk). Excavate some crevices and push in compost, pop seeds in a fold of paper and blow them in. Mist with a fine spray and then hold in place with a wad of damp loo paper. Fern plants, such as Asplenium adiantum-nigrum and A. trichomanes, should be stuffed in root first. A drip water irrigation system in the top of the wall will help plants establish, or water regularly but carefully to avoid dislodging them.

I have a small balcony of brick and metal that I would like to cover with a fast-growing, hardwearing plant that won't take over the building and is safe for cats to nibble.

Start by providing something specifically for your cats. A container of turf, or of wheat or oat seedlings, will be great for them to chew on, particularly if they don't get out into the big wide world much. They also love catmint (obviously), as well as related herbs, such as thyme. The chances of them choosing to eat hazardously large quantities of any other plants when these treats are on offer are slim. However, there are some climbers that are noted for their toxicity to animals, so should probably be avoided – these include ivies and climbing hydrangeas. Clematis, too, are questionable. Among climbers, honeysuckles are considered safe. Coral honeysuckle (Lonicera sempervirens) has fantastic, hot pink flowers in summer and is pretty compact, growing to about 12ft. It also may be evergreen in milder winters. Grow your honeysuckle in a large pot, and erect a set of wires or a trellis for it to climb over, tying it in regularly. You don't mention your aspect, but honeysuckles have the added benefit that they will grow and flower well in shade.

We have an almost sheer bank down one side of our driveway. It is mud, rock and weeds covered by a plastic mesh, and is south-facing. The bank is hard to reach – what can we grow to cover it all year that will need only minimal maintenance?

Any plant will work better than the mesh. Roots are great at binding soil together and stopping it washing away. If you choose something with dense enough growth, it will also keep the weeds down. Evergreen ground cover for a sunny spot includes: spiky blue conifer Juniperus horizontalis, fuzzy-foliaged Stachys lanata, the variegated periwinkle, Vinca major 'Variegata' and the black-leaved grass Ophiopogon planiscapus 'Nigrescens'. You could also try Lonicera ' Halliana', the evergreen honeysuckle.

What to do this week

Left to grow, weeds will nick all the moisture from around your vegetable plants' roots and smother their light. Your attentions are all that stand between your beloved plants and a weedy grave. There are two types of weed: perennials and annuals. Annuals are easy – you just hoe them or pull them out of the ground, ideally before they flower and set seed and cause any more trouble. Perennial weeds are different. You can chop the tops off bindweed, dandelions and horsetail for years and they will keep bouncing back, zombie-like, due to their network of horrendously persistent roots. For good perennial weed control you have to clear the whole bed before planting, pulling out every root, and then guard against encroachment by digging trenches and inserting boards.

Forsythias can go feral if left to their own devices. Rein them in now, just after flowering. Take out about a third of the stems down to the base, then prune other stems back by up to a third, as you see fit. Some people prefer the 'council contractor's chop' and try to grow it as a formal hedge. A forsythia hedge will always be a struggle against nature, but if such cubes of yellow float your boat, prune it now. Neaten up growth towards the end of summer, too, and cut out some of the inner stems every now and then to encourage new growth.

It's time to bring strawberries in pots into a greenhouse, a polytunnel or a warm, sheltered spot. They need winter chill to flower well, but now you can mollycoddle them into producing early fruit. Feed with tomato fertiliser and, once flowers appear, they will need pollinating, so leave greenhouse doors open by day.

Early April

Last season, I failed miserably with my leafy greens from seed, such as Pentland Brig kale and spinach beet. My garden has numerous seed-eating birds, and the seed rows were rapidly obliterated by weeds. How can I get a good crop without the use of a cold frame or greenhouse?

There are two ways around this. The obvious solution is to start them off in pots (perhaps in basic plastic propagator trays with transparent covers) and transplant them once they are small plants. This sidesteps the bird problem, and the transplanted seedlings should be easy to distinguish from the weeds. However, I have been told that it's better to sow seeds of winter brassicas (kale, brussels sprouts, sprouting broccoli) direct into the soil, as this allows them to put down a deep tap root, which helps keep them stable during bad winter weather. (For similar reasons you must not feed and water them too much: they need to be toughened up in preparation for winter onslaughts). So you could try the 'stale seedbed' technique. This involves digging over your soil and then leaving it until the weeds germinate. You then hoe them off, taking care to disturb the soil as little as possible, before sowing your seeds. Then cover the whole thing with fleece: this will keep the birds away and protect the kale from flea beetle and cabbage whites later on, while protecting the spinach beet from frosts. Tardy gardeners take note: all of the winter brassicas have a long growing season and need to be well under way by the end of this month.

I bought some agapanthus bulbs last year and was very disappointed when, out of 15, only one produced flowers. Will they never flower?
Agapanthus hates to be moved, and often takes at least a year to flower after being planted, so don't be too surprised if you get nothing this year either. You must give the newly planted bulbs time

to settle in, no matter how pathetic they seem. We expect so much from them in their first year, but it is a blessing if they don't flower. It means they are putting down roots and bulking themselves up, rather than wasting their energies on fripperies such as flowers. They will be better plants for it in the long run.

I have a 20-year-old ivy on my house. This month it developed a black, soot-like mould and there are cream insect larvae embedded in the leaves. I don't know whether to spray with systemic fungicide in case it affects the birds nesting there.

Step away from the fungicide. You must never, ever mess with a nesting bird. Ethics (and the law) aside, they show you have a healthy ecosystem likely to include beneficial insects such as ladybirds and lacewings. These are voracious consumers of scale insects, which is what you have – the mould is a side-effect. These pests get the upper hand at this time of year, but give it a month or so until the beneficial insects hit their stride. If you must act, boost ladybird and lacewing populations with a breeding kit from greengardener.co.uk.

The previous owner cemented over most of our small garden. We would like to replace it with pebbles. Do we need planning permission? A specialist builder? And how much will it cost?

You don't need planning permission or a specialist builder. If you're going for pebbles (I hope you mean tiny, gravel-like ones, otherwise they're impossible to walk on), you may not even have to do much at all, just buy in a few tonnes and lob them on. Laying honeycomb rubber matting first, which holds the gravel in small pockets, will prevent scuffed bald patches (fieldguard.com/safe_surfaces.html). Also consider moving the concrete. A landscaper may do it for you, if they're pushed for work, but you may have more luck with builders. And if you're fit, you could do it yourself, hiring a breaker and a skip into which to chuck it all. Cost depends on your area, but it is going to take a couple of strong young things two days, plus a skip, so most probably around the £750 mark.

I have planted a Rhododendron yakushimanum in my small London garden and the leaves have yellowed. I read it could be iron deficiency.

It is iron and manganese deficiency. The problem is not a lack in the soil – there will be plenty – but that rhododendrons struggle to absorb nutrients when the soil is not at the correct pH level. Rhododendrons like acidic soil, and you haven't got it. A sprinkle of sulphur chips will help acidify the soil, as will regular applications of a rhododendron and azalea fertiliser. But you are fighting a losing battle. Even in a container of ericaceous compost it is tricky to maintain the correct pH. In the soil it is almost impossible. Far simpler to choose plants suited to your soil type, which is just about everything but rhododendrons.

Could you advise me how and when to prune a lilac? Is it really possible that it might die when pruned?

There's a lot of rubbish talked about pruning, usually making it seem more mysterious than it is. You won't kill your lilac by pruning it. You could, I suppose, give it a shock if you cut it down to the ground just prior to a hard frost, but it would still survive. If needs must, you can prune most things whenever and however, as long as you are prepared for them to look a bit funny or don't mind sacrificing some flowers. The finer points are about maximising flowering and creating a good shape so wait until after it has flowered in spring, or you will be lopping off flower buds that it has worked all year to make. Then, if it is overgrown, carry out renovation pruning by removing the oldest and woodiest third of the stems right back to the base. Do the same the following spring with another third, and the next year with the final third. Routine pruning involves removing the spent flowers each year as soon as they have faded, and cutting back into the wood a little, to a bud.

What to do this week

You can pot up lily bulbs now to slip nonchalantly into gaps in your border later on or, even simpler, just plant those that need no such cosseting straight into the ground. The Asiatic hybrids, such as blood-red 'Marrakech', greeny-yellow 'Medallion' and orange 'Fire King', are not the best-scented of lilies, but they are reliable, coming up year after year, and the clump increases in size, too. Add grit to the planting hole and plant at two-and-a-half times the bulb's depth.

Any plant that has mysteriously refused to flower in previous years (despite being otherwise in rude health) may just need feeding. Avoid general feeds – a handful of sulphate of potash can produce miraculously floriferous results. Sprinkle it around fruit trees, strawberries and any flowering and fruiting plants, then work it in with a rake and water well. Do this every month throughout summer to restore your green fingers.

Peaches and nectarines produce the first of the blossoms and they are hugely welcome, but in lifting our winter-worn spirits they put themselves at some peril. There is still a real risk of a frost and if they get hit just once, you could lose your whole crop for this year. Keep a swathe of horticultural fleece to hand, and a keen eye on the weather reports, and be prepared to dash out and tuck yours in at the first sign of a drop in temperature.

Mid April

I have a three-year-old acer that is supported with a stake. When is it desirable to remove the support?

Stakes are necessary to begin with, because newly-planted trees have such reduced root systems that they would simply keel over at the first breeze. It is equally important, however, to remove them fairly early, otherwise the tree can become dependent on them. A good guide is to give the tree one full growing season with the support, and then remove it at the beginning of spring the following year – by autumn, the tree will have put out lots of supporting roots. Yours was most probably ready to fend for itself a while ago and spring is a good time to remove the stake. Older trees should have their stakes reduced each spring over a few years, to give them a chance to adjust.

Why can't I grow basil? I have no problems germinating the seed, but the seedlings seem to hate being transplanted. Year after year the plants come to nothing, whether left in pots or put out in the garden.

Are you hardening them off properly? Basil gets a shock if moved from toasty windowsill to chilly outdoors. Hardening off needs to be slow: first to a closed cold frame, then with the lid slightly ajar by day and closed by night, then open both day and night, before, finally, moving to the garden. And it mustn't be too soon: if you're not happy sitting out at night, neither is basil, so wait well into May. In June and July, you can sow direct into open ground: then you'll get fantastic crops with no transplant shock.

I have a small front garden (3m x 6m) and want a tree to attract birds and provide privacy. The hedge (on three sides) is in poor condition because a local cat jumps through it.

You have just enough space to squeeze in a small tree. For wildlife, go for a native, or at least a relative of a native. Hawthorn 'Plena' is a highfalutin, double-flowered version of the basic hedgerow plant, with red berries in autumn. Crab apples offer an outstanding crop-to-plant-size ratio, and 'John Downie' is bountiful, dripping with orange-red fruit in autumn. Don't change your hedge: birds love them. Chop back, feed, water and mulch, and see if its looks improve. Mesh would keep out the cat and allow gaps to regrow.

Two years ago, I bought a Trachelospermum 'Golden Memories', choosing it carefully for its position (east-facing, sheltered). It has grown well and looks healthy but has not produced a single flower.

It doesn't sound as if there is a problem with its growing conditions, but there are a couple of things you might try to encourage flowers. Trachelospermums flower on short lateral branches produced on old wood. If yours is growing fairly vigorously, it may be producing lots of lush growth at the ends of the branches at the expense of these stockier, flower-carrying side shoots. Once the plant starts into growth in spring, pinch out the tips of the branches to encourage growth further down the plant. Avoid general feeds and instead try a dose of a potash-rich fertiliser such as one for tomatoes.

I have in my greenhouse a mature grapevine that gets covered in powdery mildew each year. Treating with chemicals makes no difference.

Powdery mildew is a fungus of enclosed and still spaces, so ventilate your greenhouse – open windows and doors in the growing season and don't crowd the vine with other plants. Prune side shoots to admit airflow and light, and thin out the bunches while the fruits are small. Dry roots are a hazard in a greenhouse and can contribute to mildew. Water the roots well and mulch. Give an occasional deep watering in summer, replacing the mulch each time. Avoid high-nitrogen fertilisers (use a high-potash one). As soon as you see any mildew, cut it off. Sulphur dust (considered suitable for organic growing) is the only available treatment: use when the buds are first breaking and repeat every seven to ten days.

We have an established patch of black bamboo, Phyllostachys nigra. I want to dig some out to give to my son for his garden. What's the best way to do this? We want it to be large enough to make an impact.

Actually, now is a good time to do it. You should take a big clump from the main plant – but that is easy for me to say. Identify your chosen chunk (a little less than 30cm across, say), then dig a trench around it, chopping off any stray rhizomes you encounter. Once you get down to a depth of about 30cm, start digging under the clump, then prise it away from the plant. Use a sharp spade, saw, kitchen knife, back-to-back pair of forks, hired labour – throw whatever you've got at it to wrench it away. Once you pot up your reluctant division in fresh compost, it will immediately start growing and putting out roots. Your son could just plant it straight out into his garden and it should be happy. Get him to dig a planting hole at least twice the size of the clump and enrich the soil with plenty of well-rotted garden compost or farmyard manure. Do chop the canes down by about half, so that the damaged roots don't have too much work to do, and then keep it well watered while it gets over the shock of separation.

What to do this week

Save yourself a fortune by growing herbs for your kitchen from seed. Chives, sage, marjoram, coriander, parsley, thyme and rosemary can all be sown now into pots in a cold frame or under a cloche, or in a sunny, sheltered spot. Thin out seedlings or transplant into individual pots. If you need banks of herbs, sow direct into the soil, but cover with cloches or a mini-polytunnel while they get going.

It's time to check what your compost heap has been up to all winter. A layer of the well-rotted stuff from the base of the heap, spread on borders and the surface of pots, will tart up the garden no end. If what you find is disappointing, however, you may need a compost activator – young nettles or comfrey leaves are good for this, while urine (in small quantities) contains the perfect balance of enzymes to heat up the heap. Challenge the exhibitionist of the household to unzip and do their bit.

The Peruvian ancestors of the humble spud have never been grown here, because these equatorial residents refuse to form tubers in our changing day lengths. But careful selection has now led to the development of the maincrop 'Mayan Gold', the first UK-adapted Peruvian potato, which can be planted until early May. Its nutty flavour, unusual, creamy texture and golden flesh have already made it a hit with the restaurant trade – from Thompson & Morgan (thompson-morgan.com).

Late April

I would like to grow some vegetables but have no garden, only containers on a sheltered step that's in semi-shade for much of the day. Will any vegetables grow in such conditions?

Loads of vegetables grow well in containers, but you are more restricted because of your shade. Lettuces and spinach thrive in shade as they love protection from any fierce summer heat. You could also try radishes, dwarf beans, peas (perhaps grown up a little wigwam of bamboo sticks) and leeks. Among the herbs go for mint, sage and parsley. Some fruits cope particularly well with shade, including strawberries, gooseberries and blueberries (the latter usually need to be grown in a pot anyway as they will grow only in an acid, or ericaceous, soil). Tomatoes are generally considered plants for full sun, but it's worth giving them a go anyway. You will get a crop but they might not be as sweet as those grown in sun. Whatever you grow, do it in the largest container you can get hold of, with crocks over the drainage holes to prevent them from blocking up, and keep well watered all summer.

Last year's lilies were destroyed by lily beetles, even though we caught many of the little red monsters. Can you suggest any prevention? Failing that, can I spray them?

Some pests cause such heartbreaking damage that I can almost understand the urge to succumb to chemicals, but there are usually alternatives. Last year, I thought vigilance had paid off and had lovely, healthy lily plants, only for the beasts to munch through the flower buds at the last moment. Grr! This year though, I sprayed the plants all over, thoroughly, with neem oil, and it really seemed to keep them away. This is a natural plant extract and fully organic, but it only gives protection for a week or two so you will need to make repeat applications. Buy it at herbal-shop.co.uk/neem_tree_oil.htm.

The two patches of daffodils on either side of my front porch have always bloomed beautifully. This year and last, one produced flowers, the other did not. I had fertilised the no-flower side with Breck's Food For Bulbs And Perennials. Is this a coincidence?

I think it is. This fertiliser has an N:P:K (nitrogen:phosphates: potash) ratio of 5:10:5. This means it has equal amounts of vegetative growth- and flower-encouraging nutrients, and a higher amount of root-encouraging nutrients, which seems spot-on for a bulb. I suspect the problem is overcrowding. Daffodil flowering goes downhill after a few years as the bulbs get packed closer together. They need to be carefully dug up, separated and replanted into freshly-worked soil. Do both sides, because the other patch won't be far behind.

I would like to plant a rose in our shady front garden. Are any roses shade-tolerant? I'd like one that grows fairly high (about 5m), is scented and not too showy. It's typical London clay soil.

You don't expect it of roses, but some will take a surprising amount of shade. The queen of them all is 'Madame Alfred Carrière'. White flowers are a magical choice for shade, where they glow rather than blind, and these ones are also beautifully scented, and adorn a vigorous and healthy plant. Moist roots are a must, so your London clay is perfect, but you will need to mix in plenty of organic matter before planting, and to mulch regularly. Madame's one drawback is that she can take a couple of years to settle in before flowering, so be patient – she's well worth the wait.

My lawn gets about two to four hours of sun a day. Surrounding trees dry it out quickly in summer, but the rest of the time it is muddy and damp. Our energetic dog does a fair bit of damage, too. I have tried seed for shade and for hard wear, but still have to reseed twice a year. Any advice?

Using a drought-tolerant seed mix could be the answer. This contains grasses with particularly deep root systems, which also make them tolerant of a bit of roughing up and even of water-logging. Look for a mix that includes a fabulous new ingredient called micro-clover, which is a tiny-leafed clover that establishes itself below the lawn and helps keep the grasses healthy by fixing nitrogen from the air and taking it down to their roots. It is also deep-rooting and so drought-tolerant. Try Johnson's Easy Lawn, for example. There is, however, no seed mix that's tough enough completely to withstand doggy damage, so I'm afraid you may always have to reseed some of his patches and gouges.

I'd like to increase my 4ft privet hedge by 12–18in. Do I just let it grow naturally or will that create gaps and make it look straggly?

It will look straggly at first, but won't take long to catch up. Let the top grow this year, but cut the sides. Next spring, cut new growth back to a third of the desired height. This will promote bushy growth lower down. Next summer, cut back twice to just below its final height. Cut back two or three times a year it will thicken up to look like the rest.

What to do this week

Companion plants have properties that protect others, and now is the time to sow three of the most potent. The poached egg plant, Limnanthes douglasii, is adored by hoverflies, the pong of French marigolds sees off whitefly, and nasturtium deters some pests and acts as a decoy for others such as black aphid. Sow this spirited trio among veg (all from organiccatalogue.com).

Dahlia tubers can be planted straight out into the garden now, but they always seem to do better if started off in pots and planted out later. This is partly because slugs love them so, and you will find it far easier to fend off their advances from the vantage point of a container. They need a fertile, moist soil, so prepare ahead by digging in lots of garden compost or well-rotted farmyard manure. When you finally entrust them to the big wide world, copper rings usually keep them safe from marauding molluscs.

If you've been hit by tomato blight in the past you may be wary of growing them again. They reach the cusp of ripeness, then the plants brown and shrivel overnight; it's horticultural heartbreak. Well now is the time to sow, so have one more go, this time trying resistant cultivars such as Ferline, as well as cherry tomatoes, which all – including stalwarts Gardeners' Delight and Sun Gold – ripen much earlier than larger tomatoes, so even if blight eventually smites them, you get a decent crop first.

End of April / beginning of May

I have a 10-year-old bamboo (Arundinaria nitida) that seems to have gone to seed. Will it now die? And what should I do with the seed?

Arundinaria is now called fargesia, and Fargesia nitida has been subject to the phenomenon known as 'gregarious flowering', wherein all members of the species across the world flower at once for a number of years. They all then die, having exhausted themselves procreating. In fact, some bamboos can survive even this, albeit looking a little raggedy, recover and eventually thrive, but fargesias have generally had it and there is nothing to be done but sit back and watch its long, slow death over the next year or so. For the best chance with the seeds, they should be so ripe they fall off the plant when shaken, but they must also be fresh because they'll deteriorate in storage. Sow into small pots of seedling compost, in a windowsill propagator. If buying a new plant, make sure it is young and of the new generation, which should not flower for 100 years.

Can you suggest a type of rose (quick-growing, large thorns) to plant in soil and troughs as an anti-burglar measure alongside a metal fence?

To really put the willies up your potential burglars, go for Rosa sericea subsp.omeiensis f. pteracantha, which has wickedly dramatic bright red thorns that they won't be able to miss. Rosa rugosa is covered in small prickles that would inflict at least as much pain, but might not be so obviously deterrent. It depends how vicious you are feeling. It makes a great, thick hedge with orange hips in autumn. The Scotch briar, R. pimpinellifolia, has nasty thorns, white flowers and deep purple-black autumn hips. The sweet briar, R. rubiginosa (traditionally used as a stock fence) provides great winter food for birds in the shape of bright red hips. They grow well in most soil but are large plants and will struggle in troughs. The stems of all are long and arching, so train them across to the areas where there is no soil. You can buy them from David Austin Roses (davidaustinroses.com).

Last year, I bought four lavender plants, three of which are almost dead. They are planted next to rosemary and catmint, which are flourishing. How can I make sure any replacement lavender survives?

Problems with grey-leaved plants such as lavender are often connected to the soil, which needs to be really free draining or it can lead to this sort of stem rot. But given that your catmint and rosemary are thriving, and they need similarly good drainage, your soil is probably OK. Just in case, mix some horticultural grit into the base of the hole before planting any replacements and take care not to overwater them. I planted two rows each of seven lavenders last year, and all flourished except one, which mysteriously pegged it within a couple of weeks. Occasionally plants have been badly looked after in the garden centre, so it is always worth asking for a replacement if they were bought recently and you think you have given them the right treatment.

My garden likes growing moss. I am not sure whether to compost it, dig it in, or dispose of it in landfill.

Composting doesn't always kill moss, but merely sends it into hibernation. In theory, it could be reactivated once the compost is spread on your garden, making your garden ever more mossy. Hot composting – where you regularly turn the heap – would kill it more efficiently. But I have to question your motivation. Moss is beautiful. Why not see it as a silky, green ground cover, suppressing weeds and sealing in moisture? There are always moss spores in the air, and you have perfect growing conditions, so your garden is going to be mossy whatever you do. I would plant a couple of Japanese maples, create hummocks of soil for the moss to drape itself over, and go with the flow.

I have a balcony with pots and window boxes, but last year wasps flew in every time I opened the window. Will any plants deter them? I don't want chemicals in my humble little growing space.

Artemisia is supposed to repel wasps, and you could avoid growing fruits or nectar-rich flowers. But plants are fairly powerless in the face of a neighbouring wasps' nest. Luckily there is a chemical-free answer in the form of the Waspinator (waspinator.co.uk): a pretend wasps' nest that fools these territorial creatures into believing your spot is already taken. It lets the wasps carry on their very important business, just not on your balcony.

I have made my garden low maintenance because of an illness. I have two wildlife ponds and am reluctant to use chemicals, but get frustrated by blanket weed and spend annoying amounts of time removing it with a hairbrush attached to a pole. Help!

How ingenious. If your ponds are shallow then they will not be low maintenance. Such ponds heat up quickly in summer, providing the perfect conditions for algae, which causes blanket weed, and it would be less work in the long run to get them dug out to at least 75cm. A pond full of debris and soil is more algae prone, so clear yours out every few years (in summer) and always plant into baskets of aquatic compost topped with gravel to prevent spillage. There is also a magic cure: barley straw. As it decomposes it releases compounds that inhibit algal growth, so fill a bag, add a brick and lob it in, changing the straw when it is rotted and black. Prepackaged products such as the Barley Straw Pond Cleaner from the RSPB's online shop (shopping.rspb.org.uk) may suit you better.

What to do this week

Sharpen up your secateurs, there's pruning to be done. When forsythia, kerria and winter-flowering jasmine have finished flowering, cut back a quarter of the oldest stems to their base to encourage new growth. It is the youngest bark of plants such as cornus and salix that is the most colourful, so if you are growing them for winter colour, cut them right down to the ground now to make them produce the fresh, bright stuff in time for next year.

Tender young plants will get a shock if you eject them from the windowsill too eagerly. Start a timetable of hardening off, looking to get them outside full time in about two weeks. Give seedlings a couple of the warmest hours of the day outside at first, then gradually increase exposure until they are tough enough to stay out all night. Horticultural fleece will help if you have neither greenhouse nor cold frame.

Apple trees are in full, beautiful blossom, but these blooms could still be cut dead by a naughty late frost. This will result in fruit starting to form and swell, making you believe all is well, but then cruelly dropping away as the season progresses. Buy a large piece of fleece and a stapler, and for the next couple of weeks keep a weather eye on the forecast, being ever ready to pounce and wrap. If you can protect only the bottom, do so, because that is where frost is most likely to hit.

Early May

I'm fed up with squirrels eating my bulbs. Are there any they don't like, or deterrents other than covering the garden with wire netting?

Wire netting can be a pain, but it is effective. If you use chicken wire with holes at least two and a half inches in diameter, the bulb foliage will be able to find its way through without you having to remove the wire every spring. It can be buried an inch or so below the surface after bulb planting, so it is not visible, but you may find this too much of a fuss, especially when you are trying to plant other things nearby. Bulbs that are supposed to be less tasty to squirrels include spring-flowering scilla, ipheion, daffodils and fritillarias, as well as summer-flowering ornamental alliums. You must always leave the foliage on a bulb until it has died down completely (to give the bulb time to lay down stores for next year's flowering), but do remove the foliage as soon as it is dead, otherwise it acts as a marker for the squirrels. They apparently hate chilli and cayenne pepper, so give bulbs in leaf an occasional dusting and do the same on the soil around the bulbs after they have died down.

I have an orange tree with small bitter fruits from which I used to make a lovely marmalade. Two years ago I had an infestation of vine weevil and unthinkingly used systemic insecticide on it. Will it be safe to eat the fruits again?

I spoke to garden chemical makers Bayer – chances are they made whatever you used – and took quite a ticking-off on your behalf. They couldn't give an answer as there are no systemic insecticides approved for use on citrus – you are meant to use them only on the plants mentioned on the tin. But this isn't because the chemical particularly lingers in citrus plants, it is because no one has got round to testing it on them. When spraying other crops with products containing thiacloprid and imidacloprid (the most commonly used systemic insecticides), harvest intervals range from three to 14 days, so I will hurl myself into Bayer's fastidious line of fire again and venture that two years is probably OK. An organic alternative (with no harvest interval) is Nemasys, a nematode (microscopic worm) you water into the soil that chomps away at the vine weevil grubs. Visit greengardener.co.uk and use twice a year, now and in autumn.

I'm new to composting but really want to get a good heap going this year. Can I compost cardboard packaging, such as cereal boxes? I'm wary of trying it in case the inks damage plants.

Plants themselves will not be harmed, but in theory edible plants could take up compounds that you wouldn't want to eat. The general rule is that any ink used to print on to non-shiny surfaces (such as newspapers) is fine, but the shiny stuff is out, which means your cereal boxes are no good. If you were planning to use the compost only on ornamental plants, rather than edibles, this wouldn't be a problem, but the laminated surface also makes them slow to rot down, so they would be a pain anyway. Cardboard boxes, egg boxes and kitchen and toilet roll insides (once you've finished using them as pots for seedlings) are all safe and make brilliant additions, helping to aerate the heap and stopping all the green stuff from turning slimy.

We have a shared courtyard with a raised bed containing some boring conifers that are getting past their best. It doesn't get much sun and can get windy. I want something a few feet high.

In the natural world, wind and shade don't often go together, so wind-tolerant plants are all sun-loving seaside and mountain dwellers. I'm not surprised you've ended up with some pretty dull plants. However, where all else fails, reach for a hardy fuchsia. They will tolerate some wind, particularly the smaller-flowered ones, which are also the loveliest. 'Hawkshead' is gorgeous, with dainty drooping white flowers with a green flush to the tips of the petals. It grows to about a metre in height with a narrower spread.

We had a heat pump installed and lost all our topsoil. How do we turn our muddy field of waterlogged clay into grass and a vegetable patch? Someone said potatoes would help.

How did you lose your topsoil? Some canny contractor making a bit of money on the side, I bet. Demand it back! Planting potatoes is a good way to break up soil when starting a new vegetable patch, because they need regular earthing up, the roots are deep and penetrating, and the dense leaf cover suppresses weeds. But it sounds as if they would just rot away in your soggy clay subsoil. You will have to pay to get topsoil imported, particularly where you want grass to grow, and this will be hellishly expensive over any large area. For the vegetable garden, you could make a series of raised beds. Fill them with manure, compost and topsoil, and make paths between them from bark chippings.

We have a Photinia 'Red Robin' that is hardly red at all and is very straggly. What shall we do? Can we cut it right back and when?

Photinias are vigorous, evergreen plants grown for their bright red, young leaves which turn bronze, then green as they age. If you have not been regularly trimming your plant, you will not be getting that really strong flush of young, colourful growth and will have been left with lots of old, green leaves with just a smattering of red each year. Your instinct is right: the way to encourage lots of new growth is hard pruning, and photinias can take it. In late spring, cut back almost to the ground, leaving just five inches or so of growth. Water well and mulch with well-rotted manure or compost to spur it on to a burst of lovely red foliage. It is important to wait until all danger of frost has passed, otherwise the young, tender foliage will be ruined. Repeat each year for the best show.

What to do this week

Almost every unsprayed apple tree gets attacked by codling moth, the larvae of which tunnels into the fruit from the blossom end, leading to many an unwary child being put off apples (and possibly psychologically scarred) for life. They will be breeding and laying eggs soon. Sticky pheromone traps don't control them completely, but they can capture enough males to make breeding less successful. Hang traps now or buy refills to make your old ones tempting again. For more information, visit agralan.co.uk.

It is hard to stop potato blight once it gets going, but you may limit the damage by keeping potatoes well earthed up as they grow. Draw the surrounding earth around the stems, leaving a couple of inches poking out. Pre-emptive strikes of technically organic but still pretty nasty fungicide Bordeaux Mixture may also help. When you first spot it – and you can relax until early July – chop off and burn all infected foliage immediately if you hope to save your tubers.

It is sadly not true that strawberries got their name from the practice of mulching with straw (they have been called it for many hundreds of years, since buxom maidens simply plucked them from hedgerows and well before they were cultivated). But it's still a good idea. Tucking a mulch of bark chippings, dried grass clippings or even straw underneath developing fruit will keep them clean, prevent rotting from contact with damp earth and can even deter slugs.

Mid May

I have a favourite camellia that has been in the same pot for 10 years and looks healthy – it seems to be in bud or flower most of the time. When should I repot it? Also, can it be pruned?

You have a short window of opportunity for repotting: wait until the flowers have faded, usually in late spring, but before summer buds have begun to form. (You are right to be concerned about the buds: they do tend to drop off after repotting.) Remember to use a lime-free, ericaceous compost every time you repot or top-dress camellias, and keep them well watered throughout the growing season. Pruning is necessary only if the plant has got too big for your garden, or if it is looking straggly. Make it put on more bushy growth by cutting back into the previous season's growth (this will be a different colour from the older wood). Again, this should be done after flowering. It can be repeated every year.

Will bad things happen if I plant sweet peas ('Matucana') and normal eating peas ('Hurst Green Shaft') along the same sunny row of fence, alternately, every metre. Will there be cross-pollination? I want to harvest and plant the sweet pea seeds next year.

This would be a fabulous idea were it not for your seed-saving plans. If you want to take a punt, you've picked the right crop. Pea flowers generally self-pollinate before they even open, so there is minimal chance of cross-pollination. But there is some chance, so you'd be best to place them in different parts of the garden, or at least to plant something tall-growing between them. Have you considered a less closely related edible climber, such as climbing French beans? Not such a good visual pun, true, but at least you'd be sure of next year's sweetly scented outcome.

I have an ornamental quince, Chaenomeles japonica, that's sending out great long branches. Can it be pinned to the fence like a climber?

These troublesome stems actually make them perfect for this treatment. There are a number of big, free-standing shrubs, including camellia, ceanothus, forsythia and your chaenomeles, that become slimline wall shrubs simply with pruning and a firm hand. The dark, bare branches and blossom-like flowers of chaenomeles look their best grown this way. Carry out all training and pruning just after it has finished flowering. Erect horizontal wires, roughly 18in apart, using vine eyes screwed into the fence. Cut out the oldest growths, and select those that are still fairly malleable. Create a permanent framework by attaching these chosen ones to the wires, using twine in a loose figure of eight. Reduce their length to fit the fence, then prune out any growth pointing in towards it, or out towards you, keeping only that which is growing parallel to the fence. In future, just prune back these side shoots to within a few buds of the framework, and remove anything heading in the wrong direction.

Several years ago, concerns were raised about creosote leaching into soil and any plants grown there. Is there any truth in this?

The greatest danger is through direct skin contact, but there is a possibility that creosote can leach into soil and be taken up by plants in small doses. It was banned for sale and use following the realisation that it is highly carcinogenic. If you have some stashed at the back of the shed, you should not use it. You can still buy sleepers treated with creosote (many haven't been, but the cheapest – used British pine – have) and you're allowed to use them where there will be no contact with children, skin or food, so no raised beds for vegetable gardening (or picnic tables, for that matter). It may also leach into groundwater, causing wider environmental damage, so just say no.

I have a Wollemi pine seedling, a plant thought to be extinct until 100 were discovered in Australia. I feel a big responsibility. Should I give it to the nearby park?

This Jurassic era relic was discovered in a remote Australian canyon in 1994. Plants were propagated and sold all over the world – more than 10,000 in the UK and Ireland alone – so although you are part of the conservation effort, you're far from the sole custodian. This burden lifted, try to enjoy what is proving to be an exceptionally beautiful and hardy plant. It hates wet roots, so as you are in north Wales, stick to the pot. It seems happy in a container long term, anyway, and regenerates well from pruning should it get too large.

The window boxes on our north-facing house get no sun or rain. The house is right on the pavement, making any plants a target for drunken revellers. What plant dislikes sun, hardly needs any water and is not at all tempting to rip out?

This sounds familiar. Where my toddler is concerned, the more established a container looks, the less likely he is to bother it. Vulnerable new plantings last minutes, but once the plants look as if they've always been there, they are ignored. Try making up your window boxes in the back garden, and give them a few weeks for roots to knit and leaves to spread before you make them prey to the attentions of inebriated passersby. Window box-sized plants that will cope with shade include begonias, ferns, hostas, fuchsias, campanulas, busy lizzies, pansies and tobacco plants. No window box is adequately watered by rain, though. You will just have to water it regularly, and every day in summer. Add some water-retaining granules such as Phostrogen SwellGel when planting.

What to do this week

Tomatoes need a lot of water as the season goes on. To help it hit the spot, and prevent run-off and splashing, when you plant out bury a piece of pipe a few inches long next to them (or a plastic cup with holes punched in its bottom) – you then water into the cavity. If you're planting into grow bags, one is too puny. Buy two, cut similar sized holes on adjoining surfaces then stack on top of each other. That way, plants have a greater root run and need less attention.

It is houseplant liberation time. They can go years without growing much, but a spell outside once the weather's reliably warm reminds them they're alive. You'll miss them, but you'll appreciate them so much more when they come back inside, clean, green and vital. Transfer to slightly larger pots of new compost, put in a shady spot, water, feed – then watch them cast aside their shackles and grow.

Are your aphids multiplying alarmingly, causing puckering and distortion to plants all around? It is easy to overreact and frantically spray, but in fact populations usually decline as natural predators get up to speed. If you feel your garden lacks natural balance, or you are just the panicky type, invest in a loveliness of ladybirds (that's one for the collective noun nerds, by the way, not me showing my poetic side) from greengardener.co.uk. There will be nothing lovely about what they do to the aphids.

Mid to late May

A couple of years ago I planted a crab apple 'Golden Hornet' in my garden. Last year it grew well and fruited magnificently, but then the fruits turned brown and split and went mouldy. What went wrong?

'Golden Hornet' is a beauty when healthy, but it is prone to apple scab, which is what you've got. The fungus that causes apple scab overwinters on fallen leaves, so you should always rake these up and burn them, but this won't be enough. You have two options, neither particularly pleasant. You could get into a fairly serious spraying habit each spring, dousing the whole tree at regular intervals with a fungicide based on mancozeb. But by far the best long-term solution is to replace the tree with one that is resistant to scab, such as 'Harry Baker' (pink flowers, big dark red fruit) or 'Red Sentinel' (red fruit that last well into winter).

I used to add orange and grapefruit peel to my compost, but then I read that tiger worms don't like it, so we stopped. Is there a way of making peel harmless for composting?

Tiger worms – the worms you're most likely to find in your compost heap – are put off by the antiseptic properties of a substance called d-limonene, which exists in fresh citrus peel. This disappears once the fruit rots, so if you cut your peelings into small pieces and add lots of other material in with them, the worms avoid the citrus until it turns mouldy. If peelings make up a large part of your heap, keep a citrus bin to one side and add the peelings to the main compost only once they've turned furry and green. The bacteria that do most of the rotting are not bothered by citrus, but your compost will work more efficiently with worms in it.

Our white camellia (C. japonica 'Primavera') was smothered in buds, but at the first rain the flowers turned brown. There's a glorious red camellia just up the street. Mine is in the same pot I bought it in five years ago.

Incredibly, a strangulated root system is not the problem here, though you really, really must pot it on. A profusion of flowers is not always a good sign – it can be a plant's last-ditch attempt to create progeny as it senses it is about to snuff it. But this is all beside the point. Your problem is that you have a white-flowered camellia, and this is how many white-flowered camellias react to a bit of rain. Pathetic, but true. The only way around it is to grow it under cover, or at least in your most sheltered spot. Or just buy a glorious red one.

I grow wildflowers, but my elderly neighbour regards them as weeds and sprays them with weedkiller through the slats of the fence. She put up the fence, and doesn't want me to grow anything near it. What can I do? Talking to her doesn't help.

This is outrageous, and the law is on your side. Mediation should be the first step (ukmediation.net). If she is not amenable, take photos and note dates. Let her know you're doing this and that you intend to involve the police – if she continues follow this up with a solicitor's letter. In truth, you may struggle to interest the police and it may be hard to take her to the small claims court because there is little monetary value to wildflowers. But hopefully she'll lose her nerve before it gets to that. Or erect your own – solid – fence alongside hers, provided it's on your own land.

My summerhouse is strong enough for a sedum roof, and I thought of using mushroom boxes to sow the sedum into – but where can I find a light growing medium? How else can I stop plants drifting downwards?

You'll need to build a wooden containment frame all the way around the edge (make plenty of holes so water can drain out into the gutters), and an inner grid to hold the mats in place. For the growing medium, I'd use a thin layer of topsoil mixed with vermiculite, to lighten things up. But you could make your life easier and buy the whole get-up from McLaw Living Roofs (mclawlivingroofs. co.uk). It sells ready-planted sedum mats and can also supply the waterproof membrane and retention strip, helping you avoid all that troublesome carpentry.

I want to replace a leylandii hedge with holly, beech and yew. Can I cut down the whole thing and replant, or should I cut down one tree at a time, replacing each with a sapling?

Leylandii's overwhelming height when left untrimmed is not the only reason they have become notorious slayers of neighbourly relations and most hated of all garden plants. Their roots rob the soil of moisture and nutrients, making it difficult for anything to grow underneath. Hedges need the best possible start in life, because they are going to be there a long time. So, if it is to stand up to future drought, disease or pest problems, you want yours to get well established in its first few years. The best start means a deep planting trench improved with lots of compost or well-rotted manure, regular watering in the first year and, most importantly, freedom from such unfair competition as leylandii. Tend to the soil after removing the leylandii, because it will be parched and bereft. If you're worried about privacy, put up a temporary screen of trellis and climbers, but don't force your saplings to battle it out with these brutes.

What to do this week

Garden centres are awash with bedding plants right now, but sneak a few edibles into those window boxes, too. Alpine strawberries and tumbler tomatoes are hanging basket naturals, while lollo rosso lettuce and 'Bull's Blood' beetroot are as colourful as any filler foliage, and runner beans (try dwarf varieties) used to be grown for their looks alone. Edibles also combine naturally with scented pelargoniums, pinks, sweet peas, nasturtiums, violas and calendulas.

Cast your mind back to last summer's perennials. Any that flopped, sprawled or keeled over need staking now if you want the mechanics camouflaged by emerging foliage. Birch or hazel sticks are perfect, or make supports using a circle of bamboo sticks laced across with string, about half the height of the fully-grown plant. Later on, spire-like perennials such as delphiniums will need individual bamboo supports to about a third of their height, to allow for a little naturalistic wafting.

If you live in the south or have a warm spot such as a south-facing slope, you can now direct-sow winter squashes. Choose a small-fruited, quick-maturing variety such as 'Uchiki Kuri' (from organiccatalogue. com or try realseeds.co.uk for some more unusual, quick-maturing varieties), rather than any with big, fat fruit that need a long season of basking. Plant into a large hole filled with well-rotted manure. Beware: while the seedlings are young, you will have to beat off slugs with a stick (or use copper rings and organic slug pellets).

End of May

What is the best way to keep my vegetables well watered this summer?

Vegetable gardens take a lot of watering, so the more efficient you can be, the better. Easier watering starts when planting out. Create dips in the ground to plant into, so allowing water to pool around the base of the plant, rather than run off the surface in all directions. You don't have to water all of your vegetables all of the time. The first important time is during plant establishment. Direct sown seed will seek out water relatively efficiently, but plants planted out from modules or pots have tiny self-contained root balls and are unused to fending for themselves, so these will need plenty of cosseting as the roots stretch out. The second priority is when fruits or tubers or pods are swelling. It is almost always best to water at the end of the day. There is an exception when it comes to courgettes, pumpkins and their like, which are prey to grey mould if the leaves are left damp over night. Except when watering delicate seedlings, you should always remove the rose attachment from your watering can and water the base of the plant to avoid splashing the leaves.

There is a cowshed close to my home that attracts flies in warm weather. What could I plant to deter them?

Providing you want to deter the flies from your own garden, rather than from the cowshed (which would be asking a bit much of any plant), there are a few you can try. The two main contenders are wormwood and any scented member of the mint family, of which there are many. They include sage, thyme, marjoram, basil, summer savory, hyssop, catmint and, of course, mint. Flies are supposed to dislike the scent, and if they have the choice between a garden filled with their fresh, clean, aseptic smells and a humming cowshed, hopefully they will find the latter irresistible. Even if you still get a few flies in the garden, at least it will smell more like herbs and less like cow poo.

Some cows recently escaped from our local field and camped out in our garden for several hours before being rounded up. Our borders escaped unscathed, but the lawn is a mess. The soil is compacted in places and the ground uneven. What should we do?

Depending on the severity of the damage, it might be best to dig up the affected area of lawn and start again. This gives you a chance to dig over the compacted parts and even out the bumps before laying new turf or sowing seed. At this time of year, seed germinates and grows fast, making a fresh sowing a cheap way of repairing damage. Start light mowing when the new grass is a few inches long. Turf, while more expensive, can be walked on sooner, but must be well watered. Lawns laid in spring often dry out over summer, and never recover. To patch up damaged areas, use a fork to push holes into the compacted ground, then brush a mix of sand and topsoil into the holes to aid drainage. Fill in dips using topsoil, then seed on top of this. And buy yourself a sturdy fence.

I have moved to a high-rise flat with a large balcony that is very windy. I would like an ornamental tree, preferably flowering and scented. Can you suggest one?

Hawthorn is one of the best small trees for windy conditions, but even the more compact species such as Crataegus orientalis (white flowers and red hips) grow up to about 15ft if left to their own devices. They respond well to pruning and shaping though, so prune regularly to keep down to size. Also try large seaside shrubs such as Colutea arborescens (yellow, pea-like flowers), which does well in wind and doesn't mind some pollution, and rosemary, to provide the scent you are after.

We have been trying to get an inherited wisteria to flower. The troublesome plant is on an east-facing wall, and according to our neighbours is at least 10 years old and has never flowered. We've pruned it twice a year, and given it potash feeds. Should we just take an axe to it?

Wisterias like a lot of light and perhaps this east-facing position just doesn't provide enough. There is also a possibility that yours is a seedling, rather than grafted. Seedlings may take 20 or more years to flower and are seldom worth the wait. Look for a graft union (a bumpy swelling) up to 30cm above the ground. Wisterias grown against walls can get very dry in late summer, when the flower buds are forming, so mulch now and water well from July until early autumn, to give it one last chance of reprieve. Otherwise, you know what to do.

I've not had one daffodil bloom this year. This includes bulbs that bloomed last year as well as newly planted bulbs. All came up blind and those in borders have disappeared completely. Are there dark forces at work?

Indeed there are, in the form of the narcissus bulb fly. It lays eggs at the base of the dying foliage and the larvae burrow into the bulb, eating out its centre and the flower-to-be. Some struggle on, but produce no flowers. Some die. Cut the tops off as soon as they are dry and fill in the holes so that the female flies, who may still be on the wing now, cannot find them. Then dig up every bulb and check which are infested. These will be soft and contain a big grub (or many small ones). Dispose of them in a malicious manner, such as burning or dropping into vinegar, and don't even consider the cosy environs of the compost heap. In autumn replant your uninfested bulbs and over-plant with some dense, evergreen ground cover (ajuga, vinca, ivy) as the flies prefer to lay next to bare earth.

What to do this week

Spring-flowering perennials may have finished their show, but they are still there, looking sad and spent and manky. Take them by the scruff of the neck and shear them all over. Youthful growth will reward your brutality and be less offensive to the eye. While you're in hacking mode, root out any lingering forget-me-nots, too, or their seedlings will have annexed your garden by next spring.

Bedding plants need regular pinching out to encourage branching and keep them bushy, but you can make use of the pinchings. Now is the time to increase stocks of pelargoniums, fuchsias and co – cuttings almost can't resist taking root when temperatures and sap are rising. Take a cutting just below the point where leaves join stem, remove the lower leaves and push the stem into well-drained compost. It's almost too easy.

Summer days and frolicking children can wreak havoc on a lawn. Grass seed struggles in warm temperatures, but fear not: unsightly scuffing can be remedied with a little cheating. Put your grass seed in the fridge for a few days prior to sowing and it will germinate as if it's early spring. You will need to scratch up the patches with a rake beforehand, then scatter your chilly seed and rake in, before watering lightly. Water every few days and more frequently in hot spells. Or just keep your little darlings inside in front of CBeebies.

Summer

Lush, burgeoning growth is what we all think we want, until summer actually arrives. Weeds grow out of control and the neighbours start giving you moody looks; vegetables run to flower and seed before you've got a single meal out of them; pests procreate and swarm all over your favourite plants. As the weather warms the number of emails I receive with the title 'Help!' increases exponentially. Summer gardens make us feel out of control, and many of the queries I am sent relate to the taming of various horticultural beasts.

The lawn is the most time-consuming of these. Once summer-proper kicks in, it really needs to be mown once a week. If it gets too long, it flops over, and you get patchy and yellow bits. It also becomes harder to cut the longer it gets. Having said that, it is a good idea to avoid cutting it too short, particularly during hot, dry weather, when longer grass can help shade the roots.

If you can find time early in the summer to put some supports in around your herbaceous perennials, you will make life much easier as the season goes on. Growth is always more luxuriant than we expect it to be, and a few carefully placed shrubby twigs now will prevent your phlox from flopping. In vegetable gardens, peas and beans will need well-constructed supports to scramble up. Tomatoes grow surprisingly large, so always provide a sturdy stake to tie them in to as they grow.

It's important to keep on top of the weeding, particularly on allotments where there are often severe perennial weed problems. Turn your back for a week or two and the couch grass, horsetail and bindweed will have annexed your plot.

The summer weather, too, is its own source of gardening problems. It is either too hot and dry, or it is too wet. In hot weather, set yourself by a good chunk of time every day for watering plants in pots. Even in wet weather these will need regular dousings, as foliage prevents water from reaching the small amount of compost in the container. Recent summers have been characterised by torrential downpours, so set up a water butt to ensure a supply of rainwater during any dry periods in-between. If you are growing tomatoes, peppers and aubergines in a greenhouse, it is a good idea to paint its exterior with shading paint to keep it a little cooler and cut down on watering.

Most gardens peak in early and mid-summer, but go into a slow decline as late summer arrives. Frequent deadheading will help prolong your display, or you can guard against this period by taking more drastic pruning action earlier in the summer. The 'Chelsea Chop' involves cutting back perennial plants such as salvia, sedum, aster and phlox by up to a half, in late May. This makes them produce flowers later, and also makes them bushier and better able to support themselves.

The rewards of your gardening efforts start to be felt during summer, but you are not the only one hoping to enjoy them. Net fruit trees and bushes as soon as fruit starts to ripen, or you will lose the lot to hungry birds. Make sure you put aside enough time to harvest all those crops that are now maturing or fruiting, such as new potatoes, broad beans, peas, salad leaves, calabrese, cauliflower, carrots, spinach, garlic, raspberries, gooseberries and strawberries each time you visit your plot, or they will quickly go past their best.

Even at this time of abundance and warmth, you should be looking to winter, and sowing seeds of vegetables such as cauliflowers, cabbages, broccoli, kale and all of the Oriental leaf vegetables. The greatest reward though, is sitting and enjoying being in your garden when it is looking its best, so don't be so busy gardening that you miss the whole show.

Beginning of June

Our apple tree is plagued by codling moths. We've tried everything – tree grease bands, pheromone traps, destroying windfalls – but the problem just gets worse. Nearly all of last year's crop was affected.

Codling moths lay eggs on apples in June and July, and two weeks later the caterpillars hatch and burrow into the fruit. Later, they crawl out in search of a cosy nook in which to overwinter. It is too late to save this year's crop. Pheromone traps (renew the pheromone each year) are helpful in that they reduce the numbers of males. Grease bands are useless against codling moths, and destroying the windfalls was also pointless – the little buggers were long gone by then. For worm-free apples next year, wrap corrugated cardboard or strong cloth around the branches in mid-July to provide attractive overwintering spots – remove and burn them in early autumn. To reduce other hiding places, scrape off loose bark and fill in cracks. Come September, try Nemasys Codling Moth Caterpillar Killer Nematodes, from ukorganics.co.uk. These nematodes attack and kill the overwintering caterpillars.

We're felling our cupressus hedging, and the neighbours are concerned over the loss of privacy along our boundary. We're extending the fence with trellis – what plants offer quick screening without blocking out light?

Humulus lupulus 'Aureus' is an elegant and quick-growing foliage plant with yellow-green, vine-like leaves. Being herbaceous, it dies down each year, so never forms a big, untidy thicket, as some vigorous climbers do. The coverage is always light, airy and fresh. A large-flowered clematis in a dark purple or red, such as 'Lasurstern' or 'Rouge Cardinal', would show up well against this pale foliage. For winter cover, grow some evergreens such as ivies or Trachelospermum jasminoides, but they're slower growing and cast deeper shade.

I want to cover a horrid northeast-facing larch lap fence with creepers, but it gets no direct sun. An evergreen would be nice, as would something scented. I thought of clematis, solanum and jasmine, but I don't want to plant something that may just die. Also, how do I attach it?

The plants you mention are sun lovers or will take only partial shade. Instead, try climbing hydrangea and Schizophragma hydrangeoides, both of which are self-clinging, so need no support and both produce white flowers and are deciduous. For evergreen cover, choose an ivy (also self-clinging), but not a variegated one because they need light. For scent, try honeysuckles, which grow well in shade, but not all are fragrant: opt for cultivars of Lonicera periclymenum (avoid the rampant L. japonica 'Halliana'). These do need support: nail a trellis to the fence or stretch horizontal wires between posts using vine eyes. Space about a foot apart and regularly tie in new growth.

Can you suggest shrubs for a south-facing border? They'll have to cope with minimal care because the property is to be let.

Shrubs from Mediterranean climates will thrive in a sunny border provided the soil is well-drained (if it's heavy, clay soil, mix in lots of horticultural grit before planting). Most are evergreen, and many exude scented oils as they warm in the sun. Pick from lavender, rosemary, cistus, sage, cytisus, phlomis, lavatera, juniper and ceanothus. Water well when planted, and during very dry spells, but only in the first year. After that, they'll be pretty self-sufficient. A mulch will help conserve water. Bark chips will do but gravel is in keeping with the plants.

Two new bay standards have been stolen from my front garden and I'm worried about the remaining tree. I don't want to change my garden, but can't afford to replace the trees on a regular basis. Is there an effective security device?

Thieves avoid plants that look well-established – they want them just in the ground, so they can be popped into a pot and sold on. Remove all clues, such as plant tags, that give away the fact that a plant is new. Gravel paths that crunch underfoot and a light that switches on in response to movement make burglars more conspicuous. As to a security device, try chicken wire: get a large enough piece to cover most of your front garden or border, and cut out pieces to fit around plants. Cut a flap to fit over your bay tree, then roll this back around the trunk, fitting it as snugly as possible and wiring the pieces together. Pin down the chicken wire and cover it in bark mulch. True, any thief with a bit of patience could get around this, but the hope is that they'll get a surprise when half the garden comes up with the tree, and so abandon it for easier pickings. This need only be a temporary measure: as soon as the tree is firmly rooted, thieves will lose interest.

Some bugger's chomping our zantedeschias. The garden's full of slugs and snails, but they've never shown an interest before. What's to blame, and how do I exterminate it?

Nothing mysterious going on here, just old-fashioned slugs and snails, though how you have got away with it before is beyond me. Have they finally laid waste to a vast hosta collection and are scouring for new prey? Whatever, try ferrous, sulphate-based organic slug pellets (Advanced Slug Killer, from organiccatalog. com) or Nemaslug (from greengardener.co.uk), a nematode that kills the slugs for you. Vine weevils also eat zantedeschias and can appear suddenly. Crushing them is the best approach at this time of year, though they, too, can be got by a nematode in September (Nemasys, also from greengardener.co.uk).

What to do this week

Here's a pest control round-up. Cats: a drop of Olbas Oil on each of several used teabags, scattered around the garden near fences and on bare earth. Silent Roar lion dung pellets are also recommended. Squirrels: cayenne pepper mixed with margarine and smeared on tempting buds. Badgers and foxes: 'scent mark' new plantings by pouring early morning urine on a large rock, log or pot nearby, every few days until plants are established – apparently they respect this and leave well alone.

French beans, runner beans, peas, sweetcorn, beetroot, even courgettes love being sown into warm soil, and should all produce a crop if sown now. Make successional sowings of salad leaves every couple of weeks. But hold off sowing carrots for a week or so: the first generation of carrot root fly is reaching the end of its life cycle, and patience will reward you with gorgeous, nibble-free roots.

The first week in June is the traditional time to sharpen shaggy box hedges and topiary, but if it's sunny, tradition be damned – wait for overcast weather or, better, drizzle. That's because light-starved inner leaves can burn when suddenly exposed to sunlight. A general feed helps them fight box blight, as does resisting the urge to clip too often: a cut now and again in September is sufficient. Use a line for a straight hedge, three canes for a cone, and a wire hoop for a ball.

Early to mid June

My lawn has an ugly circular patch where the grass does not grow. I have dug it up twice and covered it with fresh turf. Each time, after a few months, the turf dies down and the circle reappears.

Mysterious. I hope you are not easily spooked. Take-all patch is a particular problem on sandy and alkaline soils, so if that tallies with your conditions, then we may have found the culprit. It is a soil-borne disease that attacks the roots of the grass, and the patch increases in size gradually each year. Remove the turf containing the patch and cultivate to 30cm in every direction (including down). Overseed the area with a mixture high in fescues and rye grasses, and low in bent grass, which is particularly susceptible to this disease (try Rolawn Medallion Premium Lawn Seed, rolawndirect. co.uk). Watering deeply and keeping the grass relatively long will encourage deep roots and make your lawn better able to withstand the fungi's attacks.

I planted several verbascums last year. They grew and flowered, but in a poor way, with a moth-eaten look. I have seen some caterpillars on them, and I left one magnificent-looking creature because I thought it might turn into something special. Is this, perhaps, the cause?

It certainly is. The caterpillar of the mullein moth (Cucullia verbasci) is the verbascum's very own personal pest, and a gang of them can strip a plant in 24 hours. The caterpillar itself is a beauty – white with yellow bands and black markings – but it doesn't turn into anything remotely special, just an everyday dull, brown moth (not that this is reason to kill it, of course). If you can bring yourself to polish off the caterpillars when you see them, the problem is unlikely to get out of hand, because they lay few eggs. Keep your eyes peeled.

I have a traditional Cornish garden with Cornish hedges, and cannot get rid of 'mind-your-own-business', which grows persistently on the walls, paths and into flowerbeds. I am reluctant to use a weedkiller because of wildlife and the cat.

Mind-your-own-business, or Soleirolia soleirolii, regenerates from tiny pieces of stem or root left behind when weeding. Even weedkiller is repelled by the shiny leaf surface. That said, the plant doesn't fare as well in hot, sunny areas as it does in damp, shady ones, so it is worth a go in such spots. Hoe the flowerbeds on a dry day, or repeatedly weed. But are you sure you really want rid of it? Would your Cornish hedges look as lovely without those ribbons of tiny, bright green leaves? Also, mind-your-own-business, with its moss-like appearance, has a light enough presence not to interfere with other plants. Learning to love it might be your best option.

We live in a housing association flat in London and have a tiny bit of garden, much of which is rough concrete. We want to cover it in a more child-friendly surface, but we can't afford decking. Any ideas?

Many of the play surfaces available require installation, which means they are expensive and not particularly practical for a small area. However, thechildrensstore.co.uk supplies interlocking 1m x 1m rubber mats, 20mm thick, which is sufficient to cushion a fall from 1.17m. They are not exactly cheap, but they are most probably the simplest option for your small garden. The tiles are reversible, and come in green/black or red/blue. The best thing is that they are very easy to lay and to lift again, as they just lock together like a giant jigsaw puzzle and don't require any adhesive, so you can take them with you if you move house.

Our neighbour is about to replace the fence between our gardens. We have a climbing rose growing on our side. Can we save it – and if so, how?

Roses take hard pruning pretty well, and your best option would be simply to reduce its size while the fence is being replaced, then let it grow back. You will have to sacrifice flowers this year, but the shoots produced will flower next summer. Start by cutting down the whole thing to a size you think manageable – perhaps a few feet. Next, remove the oldest of the shoots right down to the base – old shoots gradually start to flower less, so it is good practice to take out a few each spring anyway so that the plant is constantly renewed and kept looking its best. Tie in the shoots as they grow and cut back the side shoots of the remainders to a couple of buds, to get the greatest possible number of flowers. Give your rose lots of water and mulch, such as well-rotted manure, to aid recovery. As it grows back, don't prune for a few years, except to deadhead.

I always look forward to the fruit from my strawberry plants, but ants always beat me to it. Is there any way I can deter them?

This will seem a daft question, but have you actually seen the ants at it? OK, you have seen huge holes in your strawberries, and ants crawling about inside munching away, but they didn't start it. Ants alone don't have the wherewithal to breach a strawberry's defences – they are opportunistic, and move in on rots and slug damage. Take care of the slugs and rots, and the ants will be frustrated. Place straw under the fruits to prevent contact with wet ground, and apply organic Advanced Slug Killer pellets (from organiccatalog.com) or water in Nemaslug nematodes, from greengardener.co.uk.

What to do this week

Figs can be prodded into greater production by shortening the new growths now. Count five leaves from the base of each stem, then chop above the last one. Embryo fruits will swell in the leaf joints, and it is these that will become next summer's crop (the more impressive, spring-formed fruits will ripen in autumn in really warm areas, but they'll be lost over winter elsewhere). Also take out one or two older branches to encourage bushy growth. You may think figs love the dry, but for the best fruits, they need regular watering and a weekly feed with tomato fertiliser.

As pond water warms up, algae multiply, creating murky, green water and blanket weed. Remove blanket weed with a rake, then leave it by the pond overnight so that evicted wildlife can crawl back into the water. To prevent it reforming, cover at least a third of the water's surface with plants, including plenty of oxygenators, and reduce the number of fish (algae feed on their waste). Visit green-ways.co.uk for barley straw pads, which release soluble carbohydrates that clump green algae together, making them harmless.

Nothing reeks like a pile of slimy grass clippings basking in the sun. They are coming thick and fast now, and the temptation is to pack them off to landfill, but please resist. The trick is never to leave them alone – mixing them into other waste helps, and the true saviour is brown cardboard, so save every scrap (one more thing that needn't be shipped off to the next county), scrounge it off neighbours, rip it up and mix it in, at least 50:50.

Mid June

My rose recently had a sudden attack of aphids. I sprayed with Roseclear, which did the trick, but the buds were left kind of atrophied. In a mad moment of spring cleaning, I cut off these buds. Will my rose flower this summer, or is that it?

It is hard to do any lasting harm to roses through pruning, and the worst you will have done is to delay flowering by a few weeks. In fact, as long as you can keep down aphid numbers, you will most probably get better flowers, because the aphid-sucked ones would have been mean and distorted. Most roses flower a second time if you cut back the flowered stems by a good few inches anyway. You have just done this early. The first influx of aphids can be so large that they can seem impossible to control. You can keep them in check with insecticides, by spraying them with a weak washing-up liquid solution, or by squishing them with your fingers. However, their numbers soon fall as natural predators such as ladybirds get into their full summer swing, so try not to panic.

Is there a remedy for bald patches in the lawn caused by dog urine? Our new retriever has made patches that re-turfing cannot cure.

There is no straightforward answer, other than fencing off your lawn. Since your dog is new, I would have thought you could train it to go elsewhere (perhaps creating a gravelled or mud area with a post for it to mark) – but, then, I don't have a dog, so what do I know? The damage done by dogs' urine is due to excessive levels of nitrogen, which burns the grass. Nitrogen is a main ingredient in fertilisers, so well-fertilised lawns may suffer more. In wet weather, it is diluted – the problems arise during dry spells, so watering the spot where the dog has been would help. As long as the grass is watered within eight hours, damage is limited, so, in dry weather, turn a sprinkler or hose on it each evening. When reseeding dead areas, choose a mix containing lots of perennial rye grass and fescues, as these are the most tolerant of being peed on.

Last year my rosemary was decimated by a splendid looking green and red striped beetle. I bought a new plant, but the beetles are back, and it's on the way out. What are they, and what can I do?

This fiendish beauty is rosemary leaf beetle, a native of the Mediterranean that is well ensconced in the London area and spreading outwards fast. There was some hope that, being a southern softie, it would be batted sideways by our cold winter, but your experience suggests otherwise. The larvae and adults simply chomp away on the leaves until the plant is dead. There are both organic and chemical insecticides available, but this being an edible plant, and one that is so attractive to bees, it's best not to use either. Vigilant picking off and despatching of the adults will keep the damage to a low level.

I have several penstemons that are doing well, but I'm not sure how to prune them. I trim off the flowers as they finish over summer, and then prune them by half their growth in spring. My cousin cuts them down nearly to the ground in autumn and new growth appears in spring. I'd appreciate your advice.

You are both doing it wrong. The summer deadheading is fine: you must do that to encourage a second flush later on. The problem with your cousin's approach is that penstemons can sometimes struggle to cope with hard frosts, and leaving the stems on over the winter gives them that little extra protection (some people mulch over the base, too, and those of a really nervous disposition even take autumn cuttings, just to be sure). If you're after a ruling, then you win, because your timing is right, but you should be a little bolder and cut right back in spring to get a full flush of new growth and prevent the plant getting too woody. Those who've failed to prune penstemons so far this year have missed the boat and are best advised to leave them be until next spring.

I love my hollyhocks, but the leaves and buds at the bottom of the stalks die off quickly, leaving only a few flowers at the very top to blossom. What's wrong? They grow in front of a fence and get sun in the morning.

Hollyhocks are martyrs to rust. Although you don't mention any of the other symptoms associated with this fungal disease, it is so common in hollyhocks, and so often leads to a loss of leaves, that it must be the cause. Very few gardeners are able to enjoy them rust-free. Earlier in the year, the leaves will have had raised, rust-coloured spots on the undersides and yellow patches on the top sides. Once these have got a grip, defoliation begins. You should cut off the stalks at ground level now and burn all of the foliage. As leaves become infected next year, do the same. You could also try growing the plants in full sun and spacing them well apart, so that the stems get good air circulation. That was the proper gardeners' answer – here's the cheats' version: grow some shorter plants in front of your hollyhocks and you won't even notice.

Last year I had a wonderful row of sweet peas, but just as they were about to bloom all the buds dropped off. I understand this is a common problem, but how can I prevent a recurrence this year? I plant them out in spring into well-rotted farmyard stuff.

You are doing everything right, but bud drop is not within your control – it's caused by the weather: a sudden cool or dull spell when plants are in full growth can cause buds to turn yellow and drop off. The widely grown, large-flowered Spencer varieties are the most susceptible, so avoid these in future. The problem usually sorts itself out once the warm weather returns and the plants go on to be unaffected and usually flower beautifully. Erratic watering is another cause of bud drop, but as your trench is full of farmyard manure, that should ensure fairly constant moisture at the roots.

What to do this week

We have been gorging ourselves on succulent asparagus spears – and it is time to stop. From here on, the shoots need to grow and not be lopped off as soon as they appear above ground. The break will help your patch build up energy for next year's crop. After harvesting your last few shoots, lightly cultivate the ground and get rid of any weeds that are taking hold. A fertiliser high in nitrogen (such as pelleted chicken manure) will provide a well-earned treat.

15 June is one of the four days of the year when 'sun time' agrees with 'clock time', so this is the moment to turn your sundial from pretty garden ornament to precision timepiece. Unless you live directly along the meridian line – hello Louth, Swavesey, Oxted and East Grinstead – there is more to it than just lining up noon when your watch says so. To get the lowdown on adjusting your sundial, visit spot-on-sundials.co.uk/noon.html, and hope for a sunny day.

In dry weather it's worth employing the 'Mediterranean mulch' technique. Farmers in hotter countries simply run the hoe around plants to break up the surface soil, which prevents a water-repelling cap from forming, and also halts the formation of those big, water-guzzling crevices that appear in the ground after any dry spell. An even tilth of fine soil allows precious moisture to go exactly where it's needed.

Late June

I have received an anonymous letter telling me I have Japanese knotweed in my garden and that it is a criminal offence to 'knowingly cause the spread of it'. I have hitherto been happy to have these impressive sprouting canes in my garden, and feel annoyed at my neighbour's nosiness. Also, I detest the thought of herbicide use on my property.

There is no law that says you have to tackle it (just that you mustn't spread it), but your indulgence is storing up trouble for yourself and any neighbours you currently get along with. Sometimes even walls and foundations can't keep it out, let alone fences. Organic control is fiddly and takes years but it can be done. I have had a letter from a reader who managed to get rid of his organically in five years (but I think he was particularly vigilant). Each summer, for up to ten years, you would need to cut the stems every couple of weeks to exhaust the plant. Fresh stems must be laid out on polythene until they are dry and brown, then burnt or – if completely dead – composted. The usual control method is several applications of a glyphosate-based herbicide, again over several years. An application now will knock the stems back so that they are ready for the most important application in autumn, when the chemical is taken to the roots of the plant as the stems die down for winter and is therefore at its most effective.

My gooseberry bushes cropped well when first planted, and have recently put on huge growth of wood and leaves but produced few berries. Why? I prune them after cropping and mulch with garden compost.

There are two potential causes. Sometimes, when plants are overfed, they produce lots of growth at the expense of flowers or fruit. However, as you give yours only garden compost, I think pruning is likely to be the problem. You don't say how you prune the bushes, only that you do it after cropping. This is the wrong time and suggests, if you don't mind me saying so, that your method may be wrong, too. Gooseberries flower and fruit only on shoots that are at least a year old, so if each year you cut back the whole thing, it doesn't have a chance. Leave the plant to grow this summer. In winter, when the leaves have dropped, select four or five of the strongest stems and completely remove everything else, including any weak or damaged wood. Each subsequent year, let four or five new canes develop, choosing them carefully to keep the centre of the bush as open as possible, so letting in plenty of air and sunlight. From the fourth year on, start removing the oldest stems. Continuing in this way, you will constantly replace the oldest wood while it is still fruiting and before it heads into decline.

We have an annual problem of weeds coming up through our gravelled parking area. Are there any organic alternatives to hoeing and hand weeding?

Not really, but it is a shame your gravel was not laid over a weed-suppressing fabric. Sometimes known as landscape fabric, this is thick and black so it lets no light through to allow weeds to germinate, but it's also porous, and prevents puddles from forming. The gravel goes on top. It is not a perfect solution, as soil will gather on its surface over time, enabling weeds to germinate, but it does help, especially with the more troublesome perennial weeds. If you could be bothered to sweep aside the gravel and lay this fabric, it would make maintenance easier.

I have a good-sized garden and would like to save rainwater but don't have space for a traditional butt. I do have a wide, low area that would fit a butt with a height of up to 50cm. It could be up to 3m long.

If your water butt's allotted space is not tall and thin, there are few options. The Rainwater Hog, from rainwaterhog.co.uk, should suit you. Designed by an Australian – and they know a thing or two about water harvesting – it measures 50cm x 22cm x 180cm, and you can put it any way up you like, including lying it on its side. It holds 180 litres of water, and you can join together as many butts as you can squeeze in.

We have three huge bamboos in our small garden. I know you can eat bamboo shoots, but am not sure which ones. Can you advise? When would you harvest them and how much can you remove without damaging the plant?

This is a brilliant way of controlling bamboo and getting an unusual crop into the bargain. I once visited Martin Crawford of the Agroforestry Research Trust in Devon. He researches the edible properties of many of our ornamental plants, and he let me sample bamboo shoots grown in his garden. They were all edible, but some proved tastier than others. The sweetest were Phyllostachys dulcis and P. edulis, and these we ate raw. Others needed to be boiled first, in their sheaths, for up to 20 minutes, but were still good. Try yours and see. Harvest a few every few days, taking up to a third of all new shoots, when less than 30cm high. Cut from the base using a sharp knife. Make shoots sweet and tender by covering them with a box or bucket for a few days to exclude light. After harvesting has finished, mulch and feed.

Can you buy outdoor artificial sun lights? We have a dark, north-facing courtyard garden that gets sun only in the morning and are wondering how to extend the 'sunshine'.

No, such a thing does not exist. Think of the bills! There are tricks to increasing the light levels in shady gardens: thin out any shading trees, paint walls a pale colour, choose pale-coloured paving or decking, and position mirrors in the lighter corners to bounce around any available light. But really, why fight? A shady garden, lushly planted with foliage plants, is a lovely thing, acting as a cool oasis on hot days and looking perfectly at ease with itself on overcast or rainy ones. Plant hostas, ferns, rodgersias, tree ferns, box topiary and glossy evergreens. And if you have an overwhelming desire to sunbathe, go to the local park.

What to do this week

The solstice is upon us, as is the moment when days become shorter and nights longer – basically it's all downhill from here until Christmas. But on the plus side, now is the perfect moment to sow short-day plants, such as oriental vegetables. Pak choi, bok choi, mibuna, mizuna, komatsuna and red mustard, which quickly run to flower and seed in the run-up to midsummer, but will grow plump and leafy for autumn and winter pickings if sown successionally from now until six weeks before the first frosts are expected.

Tomatoes are growing strongly now, but they need to be kept on the straight and narrow. Tie them into a sturdy cane or post. Side shoots that emerge from the leaf joints should be nipped off, otherwise the plant will start lumbering off in all sorts of wild directions. However, if you have a greenhouse, it is worth letting these side shoots grow a couple of inches long before you remove them. Push them into a small pot of soil, and they will take root and produce a late crop.

It's nice to feed the birds, but it's taking things a bit far to sacrifice your hard-won cherries and berries to them. Avoid the heartbreak by chucking some net over them (plants, not birds). Sold variously as fruit cage netting or bird netting, it can just be draped over, although the ideal would be a specially constructed fruit cage to keep our feathered friends at a safe distance.

End of June / beginning of July

Our new house has a small garden wall to the front, and passers-by sit on it and chat outside our front window. The noise late at night is waking up our new baby and its weary parents. What could we plant next to the wall to provide a prickly reminder to move on?

Any plant covering the wall would probably discourage sitting, but as the precious sleep of new parents is at stake here, it is worth pulling out the thorns, as it were. Many climbing roses would be too vigorous, but several of David Austin's English Roses (davidaustinroses.com) are halfway between shrub rose and climber. With arching stems but not too strong in growth, one might easily be trained over the wall and on to a sturdy trellis attached along the wall front. 'Gertrude Jekyll' has fully double pink flowers, the perfect old rose fragrance and plenty of thorns. Also consider golden yellow 'Graham Thomas' and deep red 'Tess Of The d'Urbervilles'. You will exchange revellers for sniffers, but hopefully they won't wake you up.

I have a mature ash tree in my garden that is a safe 10m from the house. However, the house next door is just 5.5m from the tree. I wonder if the roots could reach that far.

It depends who you want to believe. The usual line is that a mature ash tree should be 21m from a house, in order to avoid any risk of subsidence or root invasion. This puts both you and your neighbour, and probably half of the neighbourhood, squarely within the danger zone. However, this is the farthest distance from which an ash tree has ever caused a problem, and so it is an ultra-cautious figure, to say the least. It is an insurance company view of trees, and they would rather cut them all down, just in case. A survey carried out by scientists at Kew gives more leeway, suggesting that ash trees planted less than 10m away from houses with shallow foundations and built on shrinkable clay soils could cause problems. That will still ring alarm bells for you, but take note of those provisos. Before you get the chainsaw out, find out about your soil, as it is this, not the tree, that makes the difference between a hazardous situation and a benign one. Clay soils expand when they are full of water and contract in dry weather. Large trees suck up extra moisture, causing them to contract further. Conversely, if your house is not on a clay soil, even a willow – the worst of the tree offenders – would not create any problems.

My rhubarb keeps trying to bolt by throwing up large flowering stalks. What's causing this?

Rhubarb can bolt (which is what we call flowering when we don't want it to) as a response to dry, hot weather, so drought can be a cause. It can be remedied by first watering and then applying a mulch to seal in the water. Rhubarb can get progressively more prone to bolting as it matures, and the solution is to rejuvenate it by dividing plants every five years or so. Dig up the clump in autumn, after the leaves have died down, then use a spade to slice the crown into several sections, making sure each has a large bud. Mix compost or manure into the planting hole and plant the sections a few feet apart with the buds just above the surface. Infertile soil is another cause, so next spring, as the leaves are emerging, apply a feed such as pelleted chicken manure.

I live on the shore of one of the old slate islands of the Inner Hebrides, and my garden is basically slate waste mixed with rich, imported soil. The high winds and salt make this an inhospitable place to garden, but crocosmia flourishes like a weed and I would like to experiment with some different ones. Are there any specialist nurseries?

Ballyrogan Nurseries in County Down, Northern Ireland, holds a national collection of crocosmias and offers 150 varieties for sale, although owner Gary Dunlop warns that while most of these will grow anywhere, a few can be a bit more picky. His garden is on a rocky outcrop, so he knows about gardening in tough conditions. He also recommends agapanthus and phormium.

I am thinking of replacing the bark on my allotment paths with recycled shredded rubber car tyres, however, seeing as I try to grow vegetables in a fairly organic way, I was concerned when told that the rubber eventually contaminates the soil. Is this true?

Shredded rubber tyre mulches can be used to smother weeds or dug into the soil to relieve compaction and improve drainage. Bob Jones, marketing manager of Dunweedin' (dunweedin.co.uk), which sells shredded tyres, says they won't start to decay for at least 50 years. And even when they eventually do, the zincs and polycarbons released are at an extremely low level. The Soil Association is yet to take a stance on this very new product, but Garden Organic – the national charity for organic growing – is wary. It warns that tyres do contain toxic chemicals, and also that zinc has been known to be toxic to plants. However, it also points out that there is no research to show whether or not these contaminants at these levels are at all hazardous to humans.

Is it a myth, or do climbing plants such as Virginia creeper do untold damage to walls? I'm tempted to dress my house in their beautiful red leaves, and have just taken six healthy cuttings.

Ivy is the worst offender when it comes to wall damage, because its roots sink into any loose bits of brickwork or mortar. Virginia creeper, meanwhile, climbs by a different method – it has tendrils tipped with adhesive pads that stick benignly to the wall surface, and has no penetrating roots. If you tried to rip a live plant straight off the wall, chances are you would pull off bits of mortar, too, but once the plant is dead (for instance, after cutting the stem at the base), the adhesive pads start to shrivel and will eventually release their grip and come easily away from the wall.

What to do this week

Hanging baskets need watering daily if they are to continue looking good throughout summer, but there is always lots of run-off – a crime when water is at such a premium. Try dropping five or six ice cubes into the top, spaced around the basket – the ice will melt slowly and the water will actually be taken up by the plant roots, instead of simply hitting the patio. Do this in the evening, to minimise evaporation.

Aquatic plants (and water lilies in particular) need occasional feeding, but you don't want any fertiliser getting into the water, or algae will bloom. Tricky, eh? The answer lies in slow-release pellets, which need to be inserted firmly and deeply into the compost surrounding the plants. This involves getting rather more intimate with your pond than you might otherwise wish to, but if you want beautiful lily blooms, you know what you've got to do.

Calabrese – what everyone but allotmenteers calls broccoli – is the most super of super foods, packed with sulforaphane, one of the finest cancer-fighting compounds. Plants are quick-maturing, and if you direct sow a late variety such as 'Marathon' or 'Chevalier' you should have crops in early autumn. Still too slow? The same compound is twenty times more concentrated in sprouting broccoli seeds, which will be ready by this time next week. All are available from nickys-nursery.co.uk.

Early July

I'm sure many gardeners share my frustration with plant marker pens. I laboriously label my plants, only to find them unreadable a few months later. Can you recommend a pen that is indelible?

All pens fade and are pretty useless over time. One of the best solutions is offered by alitags.co.uk. Its labels are made of aluminium and you write on them using an HB pencil. The pencil mark reacts with the aluminium and becomes sealed in, staying legible for about thirty years. These labels are also handy for kitchen gardeners or those who grow lots of different annuals, because you can rub the name off the label using an ordinary India rubber, within one year. After that, it becomes permanent. There are lots of designs to choose from, depending on your needs and how fancy you want your plants to look. The company also sells copper labels that you can permanently score using a ballpoint pen, and that gradually turn a beautiful verdigris.

I am a student in Edinburgh and in September I'm moving to a flat with a large, unkempt garden. Our landlord says we can do what we like with it. What will provide quick results?

Neighbours of student houses everywhere applaud you. Your best bet for a quick garden that you can later abandon is to concentrate on vegetables. Even if you stay in the flat for the whole academic year, that takes you up only until next June, which is not the easiest growing season. Ideally, you'd start work now, sowing chard, oriental leaves and mustards, purple-sprouting broccoli, kale and spring cabbage in pots, to plant out in September. But dragging your worldly goods around the country is tricky enough without a vegetable garden in tow, so club together with your flatmates and buy a small vegetable pack from rocketgardens.co.uk. It's not cheap, but you will receive perfect specimens of the above veg, and more in October.

Alternatively, sow carrots, broad beans, spring onions, winter lettuce and corn salad the moment you move into your new digs. Cloches will ward off the worst of the Edinburgh winter.

My parents struggle with heavy, almost permanently soggy soil in their garden. It is too wet to cut the grass and reeds have started to grow. Drains and sumps haven't helped, and they wonder about gravel or decking.

The reeds should give you a clue. Do away with the impossible lawn and make the whole thing into a big, beautiful bog garden. Huge, rhubarb-leaved Gunnera manicata, Rodgersia, pure white arum lilies and the Himalayan blue poppy, Meconopsis , will all thrive in these conditions, along with hostas, primulas, ligularias, yellow flag iris and red Lobelia cardinalis. Many ferns such as royal (Osmunda) and ostrich (Matteuccia) will make themselves at home, as will pollarded or coppiced willows and dogwoods. Gravel is a terrible idea, but decking isn't (always). You might even consider making a 'floating' deck and walkway over the swamp, on which your parents can position pots of their favourites.

My 25-year-old wisteria flowered well last year and formed many more seed pods than usual. This year, there has been no growth at all, though two layered stems from the main plant are showing normal, healthy growth. What's going on?

I am afraid it has suffered from sudden death caused by the failure of the graft. Most wisteria plants are propagated from cuttings grafted on to a rootstock. Occasionally, the graft can fail, even so long after planting. This cuts off the plant's only source of water and nutrients, and so it dies, but any stems that have formed their own roots (such as your layered ones) survive. The impressive flurry of activity last year was the plant desperately attempting to propagate itself in its death throes. The good news is that there is nothing wrong with the soil, so you could plant another wisteria in its place. The layered stems may take years to start producing flowers, but at least they will never suffer the same fate.

I have a 10ft length of delicious autumn raspberries that is sending up runners all over the place, often more than 10ft away in the lawn. How do I keep them in check?

Raspberries are invasive plants. On a bare patch, such wanderers are a nice bonus, but they're not so much fun in lawns, or neighbours' shrubberies, for that matter. If you are going to grow them, treat them as you would any invasive plant (bamboo or mint, say) and put a barrier around the roots. Big Plant Nursery (bigplantnursery.co.uk) sells a bamboo root barrier that is a little excessive at 50cm deep (raspberries need one of only 20cm), but it will do the job. Regular mowing kills most lawn weeds, but not raspberries. Runners should be shallow-rooted, though, so can be dug up.

I live in a basement flat on a busy road and am struggling to find plants that will cope with shade and pollution. I have laurel, camellia and ivy. Can you suggest any climbers and something that flowers?

If I fulfil your entire brief, you are going to end up with a number of common types, the sort of plants that get everywhere. Kerria and forsythia will both provide flowers and can be trained up the wall as if they were climbers. Cultivars of the far more lovely Chaenomeles speciosa will do well given the same treatment. Hydrangea macrophylla will provide flowers, as will Vinca major. Mind you, Vinca would probably survive a nuclear holocaust, and I'd think twice before introducing it to my garden. If I were you, I would forget the flowers altogether and go for a cool green scheme with box shapes, fatsias and ferns. Either way, you must have the sophisticated but surprisingly robust Sarcococca confusa, with its tiny, white, beautifully scented winter flowers.

What to do this week

Bedding pots and hanging baskets are motoring along now, but this is the moment when the juice starts to run low. Most composts contain enough slow-release fertiliser to keep plants going for between four and six weeks, so depending on how prompt you were potting them up, yours may need a top-up. These mini-plantations are so densely planted that you will need to whip out the liquid fertiliser at least once a fortnight, from now until the end of summer.

Messy areas of grass containing spring bulbs can be mown down to a few inches now, as long as the bulb foliage has completely died. Cut shorter for the rest of the summer to take those rough grasses down a peg or two. After the first cut, leave the clippings lying for a few days so that any wildflower seeds drop out. If your rough patch is all grass and bulbs, remedy this by sowing seed of cowslips and fritillaries in a shady cold frame (try chilternseeds.co.uk).

If you are a keen and prompt deadheader, you may not know if you have a good hip-producing rose in your garden. Hips are not just for the wild, untamed types. 'Buff Beauty' has many little bright orange hips, 'Penelope' fat pinky ones, while those of 'Bonica' are tomato-coloured. The drawback to all this autumn bounty is that you will sacrifice later summer flowers as you let the plant set seed. If you think it's worth a go for the hips' ornamental value or for making a sweet and vitamin-packed syrup, stop deadheading now, and wait to see what autumn brings.

Mid July

I've just moved to a new house (built in 1998) and the back garden looks as if it is just a load of topsoil with grass seed scattered on it. Books recommend preparing a garden in autumn. What can I do now, apart from mowing the 'lawn'?

You can do anything at any time, but since you have the benefit of a little breather before the ideal planting and seed-sowing season, take time to do the more boring preparation tasks thoroughly. First, plan the basics: paths, borders, lawn. Clear the lawn and dig the whole area over to a spade's depth, pull out all weed roots and add lashings of well-rotted manure to future borders, and topsoil to the future lawn, to compensate for that rubbishy, new-build soil. You might even consider getting your paths laid now. This way, come autumn, you can scatter lawn seed and plant plants into a rich, welcoming, weed-free environment. Autumn and winter rains will help them get their roots down and next summer they'll grow away with happy abandon.

A plant pot on my patio has been invaded by ants. What is the best way to get rid of them?

Ants should not always be seen as a problem, as they eat some pests and in normal garden situations are useful in aerating the soil. However, in the confined space of a pot they are pretty pesky, as they create air pockets next to roots, which can dry them out and lead to the plant collapsing. They also have a habit of 'farming' aphids for the honeydew they secrete, moving them around from plant to plant and protecting them from predators, which is hardly endearing. A simple and organic solution would be to submerge the whole pot in water, for at least twenty minutes. Ants often build their nests in the damp area where the pot meets the patio, so raise yours off the ground using pot feet – this will keep the area dry and make it less attractive. A biological control is also available – Just Ants (from just-green.com) contains a nematode that does not kill the ants, but irritates them into moving elsewhere. In tests they have moved fairly far away and tend not to reappear on the same lawn.

I have a small, second-floor balcony near the sea. I bought loads of plants last winter, which died almost immediately. Then in early spring, the same thing happened again. I would like brightly coloured flowers that could stay out all year, and a climber.

With such conditions you can't go about buying plants willy-nilly. You need the most salt- and wind-tolerant toughies. Get an agapanthus, such as 'Blue Giant', and a crocosmia – 'Firebird' with bright red flowers or 'Burford Bronze' with yellow. Hardy geraniums may be man enough, and there are loads to choose from in shades of white, pink, purple and blue. Sea holly (such as Eryngium bourgatii 'Oxford Blue') will shrug off salt spray and will even provide a beautiful winter skeleton, if it doesn't get blown away. If you like bright flowers, you'll love succulent Mesembryanthemum. Climbers are trickier, but try honeysuckle.

I've heard the UK frog population is declining and that garden ponds have become important breeding grounds. Can I make a suitable pond from a half barrel, and if so, how?

Frogs, toads and newts will breed in small bodies of water, and a half-barrel is definitely good enough. Line it with pond liner and leave it to fill with rainwater. Barrels have steep sides that could trap unwary creatures, so make ramps from stones or wood both inside and out. Include some oxygenators and some floating plants – dwarf papyrus would make nice vertical growth to one side. But bear in mind that such a small area will heat up and freeze faster than a large body of water. Use barley straw pond pads in summer to control algae (green-ways.co.uk) and float a tennis ball on the surface in winter. Let the critters find their own way – you will be surprised how quickly it is colonised.

My plants are being destroyed by greenfly, and the undersides of the leaves are covered in eggs. I'd prefer not to spray with chemicals. Is there an ecological alternative?

You may have one on the go already. Greenfly lay eggs only right at the end of the season, to overwinter; in summer, they give birth to live young. So if your eggs are white and oval-shaped, they may be those of the hoverfly, which feed on greenfly. The adults often lay them among colonies of greenfly, so that they have a source of food on hatching. If they are yellow and shiny, they will be the eggs of ladybirds, just as good at chomping through the baddies. In the meantime, you could squash the aphids with your fingers, or spray them with a weak detergent solution, taking care not to spray the eggs. To encourage future colonies of beneficial insects, grow coriander, calendula, fennel, poached egg plants and feverfew, all of which are good sources of pollen for the adults. Both hoverflies and ladybirds overwinter in hollow stems, so if you have any suitable plants growing in the garden, snip off the flower heads and leave the stems until spring. Alternatively, tie a cluster of bamboo canes together and place in a dry, sheltered spot.

I have a strong, healthy jasmine growing against a fence that has lots of new shoots coming up from the base. Can I turn these into new plants?

You don't say what type of jasmine you have, but it doesn't really matter for our purposes, as they are all propagated in much the same way. If you can carefully dig up the suckers from the base, with roots attached, and pot them into fresh potting compost, they will make perfect, new little plants, with a bit of nurturing. You can also take cuttings at this time of year; they should be about 6 inches long, with the leaves from the lower two thirds removed. Push into a pot of seed and cutting compost, and cover with a clear plastic bag until new shoots appear.

What to do this week

The year's second generation of carrot fly is about to hatch, so if you've got away with leaving carrots exposed so far, it's time to give them some protection. Mini polytunnels covered in Enviromesh would do it, or you can harness the flies' own stupidity by erecting a barrier about 70cm tall either side of the row. When carrot flies reach a vertical barrier, they don't fly over or around it but ricochet off in another direction entirely. Dafties.

Fruit trees are bursting with tiny future fruits In July, but without a little thinning out, they will turn out measly and insignificant, rather than fat and juicy. Take off any damaged or diseased fruits first. Then, using a pointy pair of scissors, thin plums to 10cm apart, apples to 12cm, peaches and nectarines to 18cm and pears so there's one fruit per cluster.

Good potato hygiene is essential to avoid potato blight. This fungal disease is brought on by a specific set of warm and wet weather conditions, and usually occurs later in summer (for advanced warning, register free with blightwatch.co.uk). It leads to brown or black patches on leaves and stems, which then spread, causing the leaves to wither and collapse, and tubers to rot. Earthed-up plants are less vulnerable. Remove infected foliage as soon as you see it, and never lift tubers with infected foliage still attached.

Late July

Our compost heap is full of slugs and snails. Is there anything we can do to get rid of them? We have a standard-issue council plastic compost bin.

The compost heap is the one place slugs and snails can actually do some good. Perhaps it's where the repentant ones go. They help break down plant materials and, in fact, some species of slug eat nothing but partially rotted stuff, presenting no threat to your lettuces whatsoever. I heard of someone who created a moat around their heap, making it a kind of slug Alcatraz, if you will, and tossing in any they came across. I'm not sure that's even necessary. It's dank, it's clammy, they have all the mouldy cabbage leaves they can eat: they are going to stay put. There is the risk that you will spread baby slugs and eggs when you put the compost on your borders, but they are easy to spot if you spread the compost on a tarpaulin first.

Our back garden has a low fence, and there is no privacy from our neighbours. There is no soil along the boundary in which to plant and I feel it would be rude and provocative to erect a fence. Any suggestions?

Trellis panels are perfect for a delicate situation such as this. They provide a sturdy, solid barrier, but are very see-through, allowing you to maintain the illusion of neighbourly friendliness that you desire. You may be able to attach them directly to the existing fence, but it's more likely that you will have to nail supporting posts to the fence and fix the panels to them. The trick then is to buy the biggest pots you can find, fill with John Innes No 3 compost (the best for long-term planting) and plant some evergreen climbers in them. Go for ivy, trachelospermum, spring-flowering Clematis armandii, and winter-flowering C. cirrhosa. The ivy and C. armandii are both vigorous and will need pruning to keep them under control

– or even remove them once the others get going. Buy them small and let them find their own way over the trellis. With luck, your neighbours won't even notice they are being gradually obscured.

I'm having trouble with caterpillars on my young silver birches. They make a pretty pattern around the leaf edges, then demolish them. I sprayed last year, but it's hard to reach the top. Any ideas?

The culprit is sawfly larvae. On larger trees, I would ignore them, but they do real harm to young trees. There are logistical problems with spraying trees, as you have discovered for yourself, and anyway, you don't want anything toxic in the branches of a tree that will be used by other wildlife (that said, though, and provided you can still reach the tops of the trees, Nemasys Caterpillar Control, a biological control available from greengardener.co.uk, is an organic solution). The other green option – and a hugely satisfying one – is simply to blast them off with a hose. Those larvae that stay stuck will pupate over winter in the soil beneath the tree, so in autumn use a hoe to cultivate the soil beneath.

For three years my hydrangea has had blue blooms. This year, it has lots of foliage but only one bloom – and it's pink! I repotted it last year and have fed it regularly with Miracle-Gro. Have I got something wrong?

It is not for us to decide what colour hydrangeas will be. The soil has spoken. If you have acid soil, they will turn blue; if it's neutral or alkaline, they'll be pink – though you can try to hold back the tide using aluminium sulphate. The lack of blooms is down to something else, though. Spring frost may have killed the buds, or you may have pruned at the wrong time, or it may be in too-deep shade. Leave the dead flowers on over winter, to provide a little extra protection, then remove them in spring and avoid any further pruning for a couple of years (and whatever you do, don't ever prune after the beginning of August, because that's when next year's flower buds start to form).

Go easy on the Miracle-Gro, too – it may be giving you lush, green growth at the expense of those beautiful pink flowers.

We've had a bay tree in a pot outside for five years. About a year ago, the leaves turned from dark green to yellow – I suspect it became waterlogged at one point. We have already repotted it, trimmed back the roots and changed the compost.

The first response when any containerised plant starts looking sick is to do as you have done and get it out of its pot, brush the compost from around the roots and surface, and repot it into some fresh stuff. You will, of course, have ensured it has a layer of broken crocks beneath it, to stop the drainage holes getting blocked with compost. However, long-term potted plants can get waterlogged no matter how good the drainage you initially provide, as the roots can get so matted that no water can move. I am hoping that when you say you trimmed back the roots, it was to ease this sort of congestion, and not because all you found was a mush of dead, brown or black roots. If the latter was the case, then the waterlogging may have done serious harm, and you are witnessing the plant's death throes. Tip it out of its pot again and look for signs of healthy, white roots. If the root ball is very shallow, or most of the roots look black and dead, it is already lost and is just taking its time to croak. If there are hopeful white roots, put it back in the pot and give it a feed – something hearty such as seaweed extract or chicken manure pellets – in this case, it is probably just recovering.

Last year I bought four lovely celandines without realising they disappear after flowering. How can I cover the spaces they leave and still welcome them back in the spring?

Greater celandine is summer flowering, so I am going to assume you have bought lesser celandine. This does indeed die down completely, but you are unlikely to have trouble getting it back. It has the capacity to become a dreadful weed, as it has in my own garden. Each time I try to dig up the clusters of tiny, testicle-shaped roots, they break apart and scatter on the soil. Its only saving grace is that this disappearing act means it rubs along pretty well with summer perennials (such as penstemons, shasta daisies, geraniums, achilleas and hostas), which only just get going as it retires. One proviso: the cultivars, such as 'Brazen Hussy' and 'Bowles' Double', are more picky and, if they don't like your conditions, may simply fail to reappear in spring.

What to do this week

How you treat your wisteria in the next few weeks will determine how glorious it is next spring. You should cut back the long, whippy growths so you end up with five or six leaves on each (cut back again, to two or three, in February). The flower buds are also starting to form, so give the roots extra food and water – you will be repaid handsomely. The same goes for camellias.

To extend your salad season, make room for small plants of endive, lamb's lettuce, wild rocket and radicchio. Plant next month and start picking six weeks later, and on into winter.

Lavenders need a trim round about this time of year, to remove fading flowers and encourage a bushy habit. A light prune all over encourages them to sprout from below, so it's best to do it while they still have the rest of the summer to put on new growth. Short-lived lavenders (in fact, any silver-leaved plants) will die if cut back hard into old wood, and will also soon look daft if left to get leggy, so a light prune little and often is the only way to keep them going with dignity for a decent length of time.

End of July / beginning of August

My house backs on to a meadow. Pleasant though this is, I have the resultant problem of couch grass patches in my lawn. Can I get rid of it, or at least discourage it?

Couch grass is difficult to eradicate, especially from a lawn, but it can be controlled. To take the organic route, mow frequently, to keep this rougher looking grass tidy, but don't cut too short because this weakens other grasses. An application of a high-nitrogen fertiliser on the lawn grasses will help them compete. It is fairly easy to stop more couch from coming in, because it spreads by underground stems in the top few inches of soil. Dig a trench about six inches deep along the meadow boundary. Either leave it open or insert a barrier, such as a plank of wood, and refill.

The rudbeckia in my garden is growing very slowly this year. I mulched it with mushroom compost in March. Do you think this had an impact? Will it recover?

Mushroom compost is alkaline and can occasionally have an adverse effect on growth if used on plants that prefer an acid soil. But rudbeckia is not one of these, so you are off the hook. In fact, the timing of your mulch was perfect, sealing in winter moisture and preventing those moisture-loving rudbeckias from drying out in the warmer weather to come. When any perennial gets sluggish, it is worth trying division to give it a shot in the arm. In autumn, dig up the clump, split it (with a pair of back-to-back forks) and replant in soil that has been improved with garden compost or well-rotted manure. Next spring they should show a renewed lust for life.

I have a very old, tall privet hedge that has become woody and sparse at the base and I need something I can plant at the bottom that will grow up through it. Can you recommend anything,

preferably fast-growing, to provide privacy, and advise how I should tend the soil?

I would almost certainly opt for privet again. It will cope with the hedge's dry shade, is fast-growing and will obviously knit in well with the existing hedge. I have seen butcher's broom (Ruscus aculeatus) used to great effect as an infill plant for box hedging, but that was only because the hedge had box blight, so replanting box would have been daft. If it is practical to plant beyond the face of the hedge and lean the plant in, that will give it a better chance. Scratch out whatever planting hole you can among the roots, water well after planting, mulch with compost and keep well watered for several months.

Our garden is a narrow rectangular shape. We have a large leylandii hedge that we don't want to lose for reasons of privacy, but it does reduce the width. How can we make the garden appear less narrow?

There are lots of design tricks that fool the eye, making a garden seem larger than it is. Layers of foliage, for example, suggest that the boundaries extend farther than they do, so make borders next to the hedge and plant large-growing, small-foliaged plants (pittosporum, acers, box). Your borders should avoid following – and so emphasising – the existing lines of the garden. Go for a circular lawn or patio, with planting all around, or make diagonal areas of decking all down the garden with large planting in between to obscure boundaries and draw in the eye. Choose a simple colour scheme and apply it to the whole garden (blues and purples suggest distance, so are good choices). Finally, mirrors nestled among the foliage of the hedge imply hidden, unreachable areas of garden.

Can roses be cut while still in bud? Will they bloom in the vase or shrivel and die?

The best time to cut roses is when they're about a third of the way between tight bud and open bloom. By the time they are fully open, it is too late, and impossible to stop them flopping and shedding all their petals (quite beautiful in itself, but probably not what you're after). As soon as the cut end of a rose stem is exposed to air, it creates a seal that stops water being taken up effectively. To get around this, and to make them last as long as possible, recut the stems at an angle and then plunge them into a couple of inches of just-boiled water for 30 seconds (holding the buds away from the steam), before putting them into the vase.

I have made my garden into gravel beds with a selection of plants. It now acts as a giant litter tray for the local moggies. I used to lie in wait at 3am and squirt them with water, but now they wait until I've gone to work. Any less tiring suggestions?

The more ground is covered by plants, the less attracted the cats will be. Hurry this along with extra planting. Thymes, lawn chamomile, ajuga and tiarella will gradually spread across the gravel, but for speed and low-maintenance, go for quick-growers, like pachysandra, vinca, cotoneaster horizontalis or a low, spreading juniper. Netting loosely pegged over the area will keep cats off as the plants grow. Alternatively, try a device that will take over the 3am stakeout. The Scarecrow Sprinkler has an infrared sensor that detects the movement of a cat and aims a powerful, three-second jet of water towards it. It should see off all comers and the cats will soon learn that it doesn't have to go to work in the morning (deteracat.co.uk).

What to do this week

Deadheading is the task of the moment: without constant nippings out, your lovely garden will quickly run to seed. But beware: dahlia seed heads and flower buds are very similar, so a dash through the border may have you nipping off all that nascent colour. The buds are the slightly pointy ones looking up (leave them) and the seed pods are flatter, hanging down (chop them off).

This is a tough time of year for lettuce. It germinates best in cool conditions, and if you sow a batch in the middle of a hot day it will not budge. Sow in the early evening, so seeds are cool in that critical period about three hours after sowing. If sowing direct, water the ground well first, to chill it; if sowing in seed trays, cover with wet newspaper.

Cure your onions well, and they will last you into winter. Once the foliage turns yellow and flops, give them one more week then dig them up, lying them on the soil for a couple of days if the weather is good. Eat the soft, the imperfect and the thick of neck, and lay the rest in a bright, airy place, such as a porch, for a fortnight. Once the outer skins are papery and the roots wiry, store in net bags, plaits or even the legs of old tights, tying a knot between each onion so that you can then snip one off as you need it.

Early August

Since moving house, our compost takes an age to rot down. It has a good mix of veg peelings, paper and cardboard, but after a year the bottom is still unrotted. Our old composter was full of worms, but I haven't seen one worm in our new garden. Is this the problem?

Composting isn't dependent on worms, although they do help things motor along. Make sure the heap is moist enough, turn it and apply an activator: urine is the cheapest, and most readily available. The dearth of worms will be down to a lack of organic matter in the soil. That is their food and sustenance, and without it they die, or slope off elsewhere. Apply it liberally and sooner or later they will appear. You will probably need to buy some well-rotted farmyard manure or mushroom compost for the first year, as you get your compost situation sorted, but after that an annual application of garden compost should keep them happy and present.

We have horrible blocks on our driveway and want to change or improve them. We would like gravel for better drainage, but have a large cherry tree, which would shed leaves, blossom and small cherries on to it. Any suggestions?

You might be surprised how the blocks' appearance could be softened with a little interplanting. The idea is this: you remove, say, every other block (you may need to lift a section at a time and re-lay), so creating a checkerboard pattern. You then infill the empty spaces with a planting medium. If your front garden faces south, use gravel mixed with a little soil and plant segments of creeping thyme. If north-facing, use mainly soil and a little gravel, and plant soleirolia, known as mind-your-own-business. As long as your car is off the drive during daylight hours several days a week, the plants will be fine. The drive will have the solidity of paving and the drainage of gravel, and you won't have to pick out each cherry leaf by hand.

I have a vegetable patch about 12m square. This is surrounded by an ancient beech hedge and there are some large trees nearby. Over the years, it has become progressively harder to get decent yields, despite rotation and lots of manure and compost. Every spring, I remove a dense web of thick, fibrous roots. What can I do without eliminating the hedge and trees?

The only way is up. Creating raised beds is a lot of initial work, but it sounds like you are used to that with your annual root-removal regime. Start by laying thick, high-quality landscape fabric over the whole area. This is designed to let water through but prevent growth and roots penetrating. Then, using planks or railway sleepers, create a series of beds up to 2m wide. This will be less work than raising the whole area. Beds will need to be high, even as much as 1m, to allow room for the roots of your plants. You'll need plenty of well-rotted manure, compost or topsoil, so look in the back of your local paper for deliveries by the ton.

This year, I grew alliums for the first time. They had beautiful flowering heads, but the leaves were yellow and dying. I dug up one bulb, and found a brown grub. Is there a treatment, preferably organic?

Alliums flower once a year. The foliage appears first then turns yellow and dies off as the flowers appear, so yours were just doing what they're supposed to do. Try growing them through ground cover, such as geraniums, to hide the manky leaves. I don't think this is onion fly (which can cause leaves to yellow prematurely) as the maggots would be white, not brown. Dig up and inspect the bulbs at the end of the summer. If this is onion fly, the bulbs will have been tunnelled into by the maggots – if so, they should be burned.

Some time ago, we cut down a pear tree and cleared the bed of rubble and soil from its base. The soil is nice and crumbly, but has some coal in it. I've dug in garden compost and sawdust from the

tree felling, but any vegetables I have planted there have not grown well. I want to reinvigorate the soil using a 'green' manure. Which would you suggest?

The tree will have exhausted the soil already, and the rubble, coal and sawdust will not have helped. Garden compost is a good soil additive but sawdust is not – it takes a long time to rot and absorbs nutrients in the process. However, you will not have done any lasting damage. Where soil is concerned, a big dollop of organic matter cures most ills. To create a green manure, you sow seeds (often from the bean family) over a bare patch of ground, typically in late summer. Once they have germinated, allow the seedlings to overwinter, before digging them into the soil the following spring. Green manures are often sown on vegetable patches that have been harvested and cleared. They have several functions: they cover bare soil, preventing weed growth, erosion and nutrient leaching, they put a large amount of bulky organic matter into the soil and they replace nutrients. The idea is to dig in the young growth before it flowers and sets seed. Legumes such as field beans, vetches and trefoil are a good source of nitrogen. Alfalfa provides a range of nutrients. The Organic Gardening Catalogue has a good range (organiccatalogue.com).

My honeysuckle reaches a certain size, then develops a mould and dies back. Can you shed any light? My garden is small and by a river.

This is powdery mildew, and it is honeysuckle's bête noire. The main problem is that we tend to want to plant honeysuckle next to walls and fences, and these are naturally dry spots, because the structure creates a rain shadow, preventing rain from reaching the soil. Honeysuckle is from damp woodlands, and all it wants is a nice, moist root run. When the roots are dry, powdery mildew moves in. Even in moisture-retentive soils and in the wettest of years, this will always be a problem if there is a wall involved. Either dig yours up and move it to where it can be guaranteed moisture (even just a foot or two farther from the wall), or start watering and mulching like crazy until it gets better established. Timed drip irrigation would help.

What to do this week

For most of the year earwigs are a benign presence – they even eat some garden pests. But as late summer approaches, they start to grate due to their weakness for the petals of autumn favourites chrysanthemum and dahlia, which they chomp at all night, leaving flowers shredded as dawn breaks. Lure them into a trap: they find an upturned flowerpot balanced on a cane and stuffed with hay or straw irresistible. Shake them out well away from the border and if you have excessive numbers, drop your captives into a jar of vinegar.

It is time to give your poor, hard-working rhubarb plant a well-earned rest. The stalks are much less tender and tasty than they were at the beginning of the season, and if you are a serious crumble addict and continue to pull throughout the summer, the plants will get exhausted. Keep them well watered and give them a mulch – if they are getting large, consider lifting and splitting come autumn, to encourage young, thrusting growth in the spring.

Everything is looking pretty fine in the garden, but it won't stay that way without a little TLC. To prevent August flop, give all of your bedding plants a little trim, get liberal with the seaweed fertiliser and keep on top of deadheading. Received wisdom is that flowered rose stems should be cut back by up to 25cm, to above a leaf joint. In fact, you'll get the best second flush if you remove the minimum possible amount of leaf and stem.

Mid August

I live in a conservation area and recently two trees were felled very near my house. One was full of nesting birds. Was this act illegal?

Anyone wanting to carry out work on trees (defined as having a trunk over 75mm in diameter when measured 1.5m from the ground) in conservation areas must give the local planning authority six weeks' notice. This requirement is designed to give time to assess if the tree should be subject to a tree preservation order (TPO). If planners decide not, any work can go ahead. Trees worked on without assessment are subject to full TPO protection and related fines: up to £20,000 for destroying a tree or £2,500 for carrying out other works. As for the birds, it is an offence to intentionally damage or destroy the nest of any wild bird while it is in use or being built.

Having just lifted my garlic plants, I am disappointed to find rather small bulbs, despite luxuriant (but dying) leaves. Any suggestions?

It may sound obvious, but the most likely cause of small bulbs is that you planted small cloves. You should always plant the largest and use the small ones for cooking. You don't say what you planted, but if it was just greengrocer's garlic, you're unlikely to get good results. Choose a cultivar from a reputable supplier – Dobies (dobies. co.uk) offers some exciting gourmet garlics. If you're sent a whole bulb, break it up at the last moment before planting, because early separation can decrease yield. Finally, plant in autumn, not spring. Garlic needs to put on lots of green growth first to fuel the later bulking up of the bulbs.

My dog occasionally urinates on my pots and I recently lost two established climbers due to this. Are there any flowers or climbers that don't mind being peed on occasionally?

Bizarre as it may sound, it is worth trying plants that are usually recommended for planting by the seaside, because some of the problems caused by dog urine are down to the levels of salt it contains. High levels of salt in the soil reverse the usual uptake of water by the roots. As salts build up in the soil, water moves by osmosis out of the roots and into the more highly concentrated soil water, and so the roots become dehydrated and the plant dies. If you can water the pots regularly, you will lower the concentration and alleviate the problem a little, but seaside plants have evolved to deal with this tricky situation, so you may as well harness their expertise. Of the climbers, two of the most salt-tolerant are honeysuckle and Virginia creeper, and you could also try the climbing hydrangea, H. petiolaris. Grape vines are also tolerant, but I don't imagine you would want to eat grapes that had been watered by your dog. Go for one that is grown for its pretty autumn foliage colour, such as Vitis coignetiae. Other things you could try include potentilla, ribes, forsythia, campanula and dianthus.

I have a ring of dead grass in the lawn, about 1.5m in diameter. At the beginning of the year, the grass ring appeared to be extra green and strong. It then died. What causes it? Can it be cured?

Lucky you: the fairies have been dancing in your garden. This is a fairy ring, and pretty difficult to get rid of. It is caused by a fungus in the soil, which could have come about because of rotting wood in the soil, a high level of organic matter, or a build-up of thatch. The fungal mycelium repels water and the grass dies. But the fungus is also breaking down thatch, making nutrients more easily available, and so making some of the grass look more lustrous than ever. Treatment is by harsh chemicals, or deeply digging it out, which is back-breaking and may not work anyway. Give regular doses of fertiliser, to help the struggling grass keep up with the greener bits, or just accept it as the magical feature it is, and wait eagerly for the toadstools in autumn.

My front garden is on a busy road and contains some beautiful cherry trees. But they are big and the garden is in shade from about 11am. They also suck all moisture from the ground, so other plants aren't doing well. Any ideas?

Woodland bulbs are good for the dry, shaded ground beneath trees. Cyclamen, Anemone blanda, colchicums and bluebells will conduct most of their above-ground business before the leaves are on the trees. If you are after shrubs, berberis, pyracantha and Viburnum tinus are all tolerant of shade, drought and pollution, but you may find woodland perennials more exciting. Hosta, alchemilla, periwinkle, tiarella, heuchera and digitalis will do well, while sweet woodruff (Galium odoratum) and monkey grass (Liriope muscari) are particularly good at tolerating polluted sites.

I've just harvested a lot of sunflower seeds. Can I eat them?

The important thing is whether you have let them get fully mature before harvest and if you have dried them out properly before storing them. When the back of the flower head has turned brown, they are ready. Unfortunately, birds will get stuck into them long before this, so if you don't want to share, cover the maturing heads of seeds with a hessian sack or a pillowcase. Cut the mature heads off, along with a few inches of stalk, and hang them to dry in a well ventilated place. The husks are almost inedible, but are fiddly to remove on any kind of scale. One of the nicest ways to eat them is to roast them whole. Soak overnight (or simmer for a couple of hours) in salted water. Roast in a medium oven for about half an hour, stirring to stop them burning. The husks then crack off easily and the kernels make tasty snacks.

What to do this week

Your container plants may look spiffing and bursting with health, but beneath the foliage could lurk a devastating pest. This month, vine weevil grubs hatch. They stay below the soil all winter, because they know where the good stuff is, and their prey show symptoms only once all chance of saving them is well past. Right now, though, the loathsome larvae are young and vulnerable. Water on Vine Weevil Killer, by Nemasys (ladybirdplantcare.co.uk), and thousands of microscopic nematodes will take up arms on your behalf.

Maximise future berry yields with simple pruning and training. Summer raspberries – and hybrid berries such as loganberries and boysenberries – should have the fruited canes cut to the ground as soon as all the fruit is picked, leaving this year's new canes to be tied in. Now is also the time to cut out any new ones that have sprung up in the wrong spot. Autumn raspberries are cut to the ground after harvest, because next year's berries will be borne on next year's stems.

It is time to propagate particularly good pelargoniums for winter indoor flowers and future years. My find of the summer is 'Lord Bute', with deep purple flowers edged in pink, and one of the few to thrive in shade, so I don't want to lose it. Take four-inch cuttings from non-flowering shoots, then remove the lower leaves and trim the bottom to just below a leaf joint. Push cuttings into the edges of a pot of compost and vermiculite and leave on a windowsill. Once rooted, pot them on.

Mid to late August

Our neighbour has replaced her leylandii hedge with a fence. She has told us that we must not grow anything on our side of the fence. Has she a right to dictate this?

If it is on her land, then I'm afraid so. However, if it is on the boundary, you need to check out your title deeds (also get hold of hers from landregisteronline.gov.uk). Look for 'T' marks coming from the boundary. Whoever's side they are on owns the fence and must maintain it, and also has the right to tell their neighbour not to attach anything to it, including climbing plants and trellis. Alternatively, there may be T marks on both sides, in which case you have joint responsibility. There may also be none, in which case the law presumes that the fence belongs to the neighbour on the side with the struts and posts showing. Here's hoping she messed up and put the good side facing her garden. If all else fails, erect a freestanding trellis (or even a whole fence of your own) alongside her fence and plant merrily away.

For the past two years, my pumpkin and squash have produced lots of foliage and male flowers, and only a few female flowers towards the end of long runners. This means a lot of space is taken up for limited smallish fruit. What am I doing wrong?

It is normal for a few male flowers to be produced first, to lure the pollinators in and make sure they can find the female flowers later, but periods of cool weather can also cause more male than female flowers to be produced. There's not much you can do, as a fleece covering would keep out the pollinators. Choose early ripening varieties in future to make the most of whatever summer we get. Real Seeds (realseeds.co.uk) sells the earliest flowering and ripening varieties which have been prolific in west Wales, where it's based.

A rowan tree I planted 18 months ago is looking poorly. The leaves, berries and branches are droopy and I'm worried I have let it dry out. I recently gave it gallons of water but it hasn't made much difference.

This is almost certainly a simple case of a young tree not getting enough water over a long, hot summer. Rowans are found in greatest number in the cool, moist north and west of Britain but once they have got their roots deep into the soil, they are very tolerant of a range of conditions and make wonderful small garden trees. I am sure it will survive – autumn and winter rains will soak the roots and revive it – but in the meantime keep giving it lots of water. Give it a bucketload twice a day, with an hour or so in between soaks: soil can get so dry that it repels water, and this will make sure it is moist enough to absorb a decent amount by the second watering. Repeat a couple of times a week in dry weather. A mulch of bark chippings will prevent evaporation, but will need raking away before each watering and replacing after.

What does it mean when your lawn goes to seed?

It depends what you want. If you are after the perfect green sward, then it means you are not cutting it enough. Regular cutting keeps weeds down and makes grass plants spread and root, creating a denser, lusher lawn. It can be interesting to leave your lawn to grow long, though, just to see what other plants are hiding in it. I have just bought a house and the lawn has not been cut for at least a month. It is covered in beautiful flowering clover and the bees love it. A compromise is to regularly mow a circle in the centre of your lawn, so you always have somewhere to sit, but leave the edges to express themselves.

Why do the herbs in pots from the supermarket always die? And what can I do to make them grow?

The supermarkets aim to make them cheap enough so that you can just throw them away and buy more. They are not designed to be long-lasting and are just meant to stay fresh a bit longer than those you keep in the fridge. However, few gardeners give up on plants so easily, and there are things you can do. The seeds of supermarket herbs are sown close together to make a saleable pot as quickly as possible. This prevents air from circulating freely around the base of the plants, which in turn leads to the formation of rots and moulds. Another problem is that the pots contain only a tiny amount of compost, and this is quickly exhausted. Try using supermarket herbs as if they were large seedlings. I had great success this year with a supermarket basil plant. As soon as I got it home, I watered it well before splitting the root ball and teasing out each individual plant, keeping as much root attached as possible. These were potted up in fresh compost, three or four to a pot, and then the tops were pinched out (and eaten) to make the plants grow bushy. These pots have lasted me all summer, and the same treatment would suit all herbs. To keep them growing through autumn and into winter, bring them indoors and on to a sunny windowsill before the weather turns cold.

We have a patio garden and would like to experiment with growing our own food, but don't know whether to use growbags or pots.

Mixed salad leaves germinate and grow quickly and look great in a pot or windowbox. Buy mixed packets of seed (try fothergills. co.uk), sprinkle on to the compost and keep in shade. Hardier salad leaves – to keep you in greens through winter – include winter purslane, landcress and corn salad. Carrots grow quickly, do well in pots and you will get a crop of tender roots this year. Oriental greens such as pak choi, komatsuna and mizuna can be planted out into growbags now, and you can order small plants from Delfland Nurseries (organicplants.co.uk).

What to do this week

Containers are particularly vulnerable to holiday neglect – having made the plants in them dependent, you can't suddenly withdraw life support. Grouping pots together (not forgetting hanging baskets and window boxes) means plants provide shade for each other and creates a humid microclimate. Give each its own tray to catch rain. Amenable neighbours are worth their weight in gold at this time of year, but if you aren't so blessed, a timer switch and trickle watering system comes a close second (try hozelock.co.uk).

Tomatoes are coming into the home straight. Cut back the lower leaves to allow in sunlight to help the fruit to ripen. These leaves are probably pretty manky by now anyway, and will be no great loss to the plant. Keep pumping them with tomato food each week, but most importantly ensure a steady supply of moisture, and don't allow them to wilt in-between waterings. This can make them fall at the final hurdle and succumb to bottom-blackening blossom-end rot.

Spare a thought for the poor gasping fishes. As water warms up on hot days, it is able to hold less dissolved oxygen. Make sure at least half of your pond is open to the air (you may need to be ruthless with any thuggish pond plants), and do not tolerate duckweed on the surface or blanket weed beneath. Oxygen levels reach their lowest as dawn approaches after a particularly warm day, so leave a fountain or waterfall on overnight to prevent crisis in the depths.

End of August

How can I prevent rats living under decking? I'd also like to know whether decking can cause a water drainage problem (we have clay subsoil), and would it be more environmentally friendly to have gravel with stepping stones?

Rats are most likely to set up home under cosier, low-level decking, and where there is access from the sides so that leaves and other nesting materials can be blown or dragged in. Using decking boards to edge the outsides will help, but rats dig, so if you want to be sure, first bury a sturdy mesh a good 50cm into the ground. As for drainage, you should fix your boards slightly apart (but not rat width, obviously), so that water runs through the gaps. There will still be more run-off than before, and with your soil you may cause pooling and flooding in other areas of the garden. True, gravel is permeable, but it's nonsense for putting chairs and tables on. Check out permeable paving such as Formpave (visit hanson.co.uk).

We recently acquired a neglected allotment. While clearing old paving stones, we uncovered the entrance to an underground beehive. How should we deal with them?

I'm guessing these are bumble bees, because honey bees don't nest underground, and solitary bees (which do) do so alone (the clue's in their name). Leave them alone and avoid using pesticides. Bumble bees make small nests, rarely sting, never swarm and are wonderful pollinators, guaranteeing excellent crops. There will be an alarming period in midsummer when lots of drone bees hatch, but take heart, for these have no sting. The nest will die in the autumn, when you can dig over the patch to your heart's content.

I have a band of very thick clay about two feet down in the soil of my garden. I have tried to put in drainage, but it hasn't worked. In one particular small bed the topsoil is waterlogged all winter and in summer it becomes very dry. I have tried lots of plants, but so far nothing has survived. Any ideas?

There do exist plants that will tolerate your two extremes, but they will all do better if you can improve your soil's moisture-retaining capacities by getting lots of organic matter into the earth. Garden compost, composted bark and mushroom compost will all help. Then plant hemerocallis, Cornus alba 'Westonbirt' and its kin, and Carex oshimensis 'Evergold'. However, the best solution would be to dig out the whole bed as deep as you can manage (ideally by a couple of feet), put in a butyl liner, pierced in a few places, and then backfill. This will provide, year round, the bog garden conditions you are suffering from in winter, and you will then be able to plant gunnera, astilbe, equisetum and all manner of moisture-loving lovelies.

I have a very healthy three-year old summer jasmine, but it refuses to flower. What shall I do? It is on a north-facing fence.

Well, really – the problems that would be averted if everyone read the label before they bought a plant. It is true that a lack of flowers can sometimes be a complicated business – for instance, plants can put on too much growth at the expense of flowers, and need feeding potassium-rich fertilisers and starving of nitrogen-rich fertilisers. But mostly it's pretty straightforward. Your poor plant needs more sunlight. Summer jasmine can take a little light shade, but it is at its happiest basking in hours of direct sunlight in a sheltered, warm garden. You've planted it against a gloomy north-facing fence. Dig it up and re-plant it somewhere more suitable.

I have some spaces that I want to fill between the tree ferns on the boundary with our neighbour. I would like something green, but have tried other ferns to no avail.

I am puzzled as to why you have had no success with other ferns, as the same conditions that suit tree ferns (shady, moist) should be good for most other ferns as well. Consider giving ferns another go. The male fern Dryopteris felix-mas, the ladder fern Blechnum spicant, the soft-shield fern Polystichum setiferum and the hart's tongue fern Asplenium scolopendrium will all tolerate a slightly drier soil than most and are considered good for beginners. Dig lots of organic matter into their planting holes and keep them well watered until established. Other bold foliage plants that will hold their own against tree ferns include hostas, rodgersias, acanthus and fatsia. All tolerate drier soil but are happier with a bit of moisture.

What can I do to encourage butterflies into my garden?

August is the height of the butterfly season, but if your garden is bereft there is plenty you can do to increase visits. They want a sunny spot that is sheltered from winds and organically managed, but they also need food and water. Try to provide a relay of nectar-producing plants; any fallow periods, and they will suffer. Think aubrieta and forget-me-not for spring, scabious, buddleia and honesty for summer, and echinacea and solidago for autumn. A container of moist sand will allow them to drink without taking a dunk.

What to do this week

Hardy geraniums have been the workhorses of the garden all summer long, and there is plenty of life in them yet. But you have a choice: squeeze the last few flowers out of your exhausted, sprawling plants, or chop them back now. Given a good trim, the plant still has time to put on a small, neat mound of fresh growth to carry it through autumn, and will look tidy all winter. Otherwise, cut back your messy mass of tangled stems in spring.

It is possible to make nests for bees, but the best will be those they make for themselves. Make this easier for them. A messy garden is a bee-friendly garden, so keep paving and decking to a minimum and leave some areas untidy and overgrown. Mulching with bark chips or black plastic has put paid to many potential nesting sites, so keep it to a minimum. Bumblebees also like compost heaps and hedges.

Lawns put up with a lot all summer and now deserve a treat. Apply a lawn feed to strengthen roots and shore up disease defences. Choose a winter feed that's high in potassium, rather than a nitrogen-rich summer feed (this promotes soft growth that won't cope with cooler temperatures). Diluted comfrey liquid is perfect.

Autumn

Autumn is a time of winding down and packing up in the garden, but don't be too keen to tidy everything away. A good, thorough chopping down and scrubbing out of the garden used to be the done thing, but it is generally thought now that this slash and burn technique – however satisfying at a time when the garden is naturally looking messy – has its disadvantages. Beneficial insects hibernate in and around dead perennials, birds eat their seeds, and mammals make use of their stems. In addition, a good covering of stems will keep the frost out of the crowns of perennials and can help them weather a particularly cold patch. Don't be too hasty; instead go through the garden selectively with a careful eye, cutting out only those stems that are looking particularly bent and dishevelled, but forcing yourself to leave the rest.

Gardens tend to fade away in autumn, but in fact there are loads of plants that will brighten the garden up at this time. Visit nurseries and garden centres to see what looks good now. Big daisies such as echinacea, rudbeckia, Japanese anemone and helenium are great value, loved by bees and other insects, and you can team them with penstemon, crocosmia, sedum and ornamental grasses. You also need to think ahead to spring, and order and plant spring bulbs. Daffodils should be planted early, by the end of September, as they need to get their roots growing before it gets really cold. Tulips should be planted late, and certainly not before November. Everything else can be planted in-between.

If there are any evergreens in your garden that have outgrown their space, or that would just look better elsewhere, mid-autumn is the time to move them. The weather isn't too hot, but the soil is still warm, and there should be plenty of rain on the way to settle in shell-shocked roots.

Lawns will still need to be cut, but the cuts will become less frequent as the weather cools. In autumn you can carry out basic lawn maintenance, such as scratching out the build up of dead grass with a spring tined rake, aerating the soil by pushing a fork into it repeatedly, and overseeding any patches.

Clear your greenhouse of any lingering tomato plants and make way for any tender stuff. Giving it a thorough scrub down will evict any nasties that have crawled in over summer. Wipe off greenhouse shading paint and insulate with bubblewrap if you have tender plants to move indoors. Keeping a full water butt in the greenhouse over winter can help regulate the temperature and prevent plants inside being affected by frost, but you may also need to get a greenhouse heater up and running, depending on your plants.

If you have clay soil on an allotment or vegetable patch, autumn is the time to dig it over, roughly, leaving nice big clods sticking up out of the ground. These will freeze and thaw several times over winter, which gives the earth a thorough working over for minimum labour. Sandy soils are usually left and dug over in spring. Harvesting will be the main job on the allotment as sweetcorn, onions, pumpkins, tomatoes, peppers, beans, peas and carrots reach maturity.

Winter squash and maincrop potatoes both require a curing process if they are to store well. Potatoes simply need a few hours in the sunshine after being dug up to dry off and harden up their skins but squash need about ten days in the sun to make them fit for storage. As apples ripen you may want to pick and store them in racks in a cool, frost free place. Pears should be picked while they are hard and ripened in storage. You can still do some sowing for winter salad crops: hardy winter lettuces, corn salad, winter purslane, spring onions and Oriental veg can all be sown into mid-autumn.

In early autumn there is plenty of food still around for birds, but it is a good idea to get prepared for winter (you should really keep feeding all year round anyway). To that end, bulk buy some good quality bird food to make sure you don't run out over winter. If you have space in the freezer, stow away some windfall apples, which you can throw out on the lawn later in the winter to keep thrushes happy. While you're thinking of wildlife, put up some homes for beneficial insects such as ladybirds and hoverflies to hibernate in.

Beginning of September

I have a garden on chalk with no topsoil. This year I have let three-quarters go to meadow grass. When is the best time to cut it, and do I rake up the cuttings or leave them?

Having no topsoil gives you a great boost. Wildflowers grow well in poor soils but lawn grasses and lawn weeds don't, so you are giving your meadow a head start against its greatest foe. In the first year of a newly sown wildflower meadow, cut a few times and remove the cuttings. This helps keep down weeds. There is no strict timing to this, just do it as you get round to it. In the second year and beyond, you can leave the growth all summer and cut only once, perhaps in September after everything has flowered and set seed. Leave the cuttings for a few days so they dry out and the seeds drop on to the soil, then rake them up using a spring-tined rake. This prevents them rotting down and enriching the soil, which would allow coarse grasses to move in. For the same reason, you mustn't fertilise an area you are trying to turn into a wildflower meadow.

We've been growing organic vegetables for two years, but our neighbour has sprayed weedkiller around his borders to kill the nettles and I'm worried about contamination – we have potatoes and onions right up to the boundary fence. I don't know what he is using, and he is difficult to communicate with.

What a charmer. I contacted Garden Organic (gardenorganic.org. uk), whose head of advisory, Sally Smith, was reassuringly relaxed about your situation. She guesses he's using something glyphosate-based, such as Roundup. On contact with the leaves, this is taken into the plant's system and, to a certain extent, breaks down on contact with soil. The main danger to your plants would therefore be from drift at the time of spraying (so the fence works in your favour), and the damage would be very obvious: they would die. Potatoes, along with tomatoes, are about the most weedkiller-sensitive plants, so if they are alive they won't have been touched. Smith would be more concerned if you had a pond, because glyphosate can affect tadpoles and frogs.

My young walnut tree (grown from a nut left, presumably, by a squirrel 25 years ago) is now showing its first reasonable crop. How should I dry and keep the nuts?

You must pick the nuts just as they reach maturity, or the kernels may turn dark and a mould can develop. Start checking now and over the next few weeks, looking for a loosening between nut and husk. Harvest all when you see this happening, then remove husks and rinse, using rubber gloves to protect your hands from staining. Leave the nuts (in their shells) in the sun for two to three weeks or, if the weather is not looking so compliant, put them overnight in a food dehydrator (available from good kitchen shops). When the kernel snaps cleanly, they are ready. Seedlings take a long time to produce nuts and they will not be of the best quality. I hope yours prove worth waiting for, but if you are disappointed, grafted cultivars such as 'Broadview' and 'Rita' will produce nuts in about four years.

I want to put up a greenhouse. An American website advised me to lay down some railway sleepers and bolt the greenhouse on to them. It also suggested stopping these from blowing away using earth anchors, but I can't find a UK supplier.

That may be the way they do it over there. Over here, we tend more towards fixing on to paving or concrete with the Gardman Greenhouse Base Anchor or similar. Much simpler. However, you have come this far so let's do it their way. Railway sleepers aren't particularly prone to blowing away, but you might conceivably get wind rock, so choose the heaviest type and bolt them together (find out more at railwaysleepers.co.uk). I don't know why it is impossible for UK home gardeners to get hold of earth anchors. Happily, the world of caravanning has trundled into the breach in the form of the Screwpeg (screwpegs.com), a drill-in tent peg for hard or unstable ground. Drilled in at an angle and attached with cable, they will make your greenhouse as secure as a caravan awning in a Scunthorpe gale.

We have three flowering currants (ribes). The oldest is twenty years, and failed to come into leaf this year. A younger plant flowered poorly, then started to die back, and now the third is on its way out. What is happening? Can I replace them?

Big honey-fungus shaped bells are ringing. Creeping sudden death is characteristic of this garden-wrecker, and ribes are particularly prone. Prise off the bark of the dead one and look for a film of white mycelium, which smells of mushrooms, covering the wood. If you are unsure, plant some strawberries, a useful indicator plant as they will quickly die if there is any honey fungus about. If I'm right, you'll need to dig up as much of the root of the affected plants as possible, and replace only with resistant ones (the RHS has a list: rhs.org.uk/advice/profiles1100/honey_fungus.asp) – so no ribes, I'm afraid.

I am about to cut down my monkshood plant. Is it OK to put the cuttings on the compost heap? I understand all parts of this plant are poisonous, and my compost will eventually go on my vegetable beds.

Composting breaks down any harmful toxins in plants and it will be safe for you to use the resulting compost on your vegetable beds. The only problem might be the effect any uncomposted material could have on soil organisms such as earthworms. So make sure your heap is composting well. I would also shred the monkshood or cut it up finely. Don't add too much at once, and maybe give this batch a longer composting session than your usual. It is more important to avoid composting plants that are toxic to other plants, such as eucalyptus, laurel, walnut and juniper.

What to do this week

Lilies can be planted any time from now until spring, but the later you leave it, the more pathetic the results will be, as bulbs struggle to root and flower at the same time. Look out for bulb arrivals in garden centres and plant them as soon as you see them. Plant in pots or into ground prepared with lots of organic matter and grit, then cover with a thick mulch (such as bark chippings) to keep out the frosts. And come spring, resist those desperately shooting bulbs calling to you from the bargain bins.

Time to sow winter bedding plants. Pansies are always enticing, with their big flowers providing the greatest splash of colour, but they have an annoying tendency to shut up shop when really cold weather starts, returning to form only in milder spells. Useless. But smaller-flowered winter violas will soldier on throughout. In trials, Thompson & Morgan (thompson-morgan.com) found the most reliably floriferous in cold weather to be Viola 'Endurio Mixed'.

First Early onion sets have been specially bred for autumn planting and overwintering. They are then ready to leap into growth in spring and yield a bumper crop of onions to fill the 'onion gap': the time between the end of the stored onions and the availability of spring-sown sets. 'Radar' produces delicious mild bulbs ready for pulling in late May but with sufficiently strong skins to store until autumn. 'Electric' is a semi-globe, red-ringed variety that contrasts well in colour and matures in mid-June, just in time for summer salads.

Early to mid September

Our new plot in Exmoor is infested with the bad type of rhododendron. I've tried dealing with it organically, but in some areas their roots are the only things preventing landslide.

This will be the fearsome Rhododendron ponticum, a purple-flowered shrub first introduced as an ornamental. Problems arise when it takes off for the wild, forming dense thickets that no native birds or animals nest in or eat, and under which nothing will grow. As the fallen leaves rot, they release a growth-inhibiting chemical, so anything planted in their wake is stunted. You can speed the soil's recovery by clearing the top layer of leaf litter, although you should resist planting for a year. To hold soil in place in the meantime, dig in physical barriers, such as logs or railway sleepers. Pin biodegradable matting (ie, coir) over the area to stabilise it temporarily. Plant trees and shrubs with extensive root systems to bind the soil together – natives to Exmoor include rowan, whitebeam, hazel and blackthorn. There'll be plenty of dormant seeds waiting to spring into life once you've put the bullies in their place.

My neighbours feed the birds, which in turn feeds a growing local mouse population. Do any bird feeders prevent seed falling to the ground? What about traps that don't harm other wildlife? I currently release mice in a nearby park, but suspect they come back.

This is the annoying thing about feeding wild birds: mice (and rats) love bird food, too. Trapping and poisoning is tricky outdoors: poisoned mice may be eaten by other animals, while traditional traps are indiscriminate. As for your humane trapping and release in a local park, you are just taking the mice out for a jolly, because they have a strong homing instinct. Remove the ready source of food, however, and they may well go elsewhere, or at least not multiply so alarmingly. Your neighbours just need a seed tray under their feeder – get one from the RSPB (go to 'Bird Care Accessories' on rspb.org.uk). It's also an idea to pave under the feeder, and sweep up regularly.

I have a lovely, thriving, 20-year-old black mulberry. The problem is that it thrives too much. Each winter I prune it, leaving horizontal spurs to bear fruit, but growth is accelerating and fruit production is declining. Is it best to root prune, and if so, how?

This is an old-fashioned technique, which was used to control the growth of young trees that were too vigorous and not producing much fruit – and it is risky. Instead, try swapping your winter prune for a summer prune. This can slow growth as it removes photosynthesising leaf. It also lets more light and air into the plant, making it more likely to bear fruit. Cut back new side growths to about 12cm, between the beginning of August and the end of September. Root pruning involves digging out the soil around the base of the tree to expose the anchoring roots. These are then cut, leaving the fibrous roots intact. On small trees, the whole tree is done at once, and is lifted to cut the roots. Larger trees should be done over two years and cannot be lifted.

My crop of tomatoes had a bad attack of blight this year. Can I compost all the rotten ones or will the fungal spores live on in the compost?

Particularly wet and humid weather means a terrible year for tomato blight and even gardeners who usually escape it by growing under cover can be hit. Composting is OK if your compost heap gets really hot, as this will kill off the spores, but few gardeners can be sure of this. If you don't kill off the spores, you will be providing a source of infection as soon as you spread the compost on your garden next year, so you may suffer earlier attacks than you would otherwise. Another solution is to put the waste in your green bin – council compost heaps are on a much bigger scale and get really hot, so you won't be being antisocial or exacerbating the problem by doing so. The RHS recommends a pre-emptive strike with a fungicide (for all you organic types, this means Bordeaux mixture), once about four of the trusses have set fruit and you are ready to pinch out the tops. This should then be repeated every 10 days or so.

Do you have any tips for getting pears down from my 30ft tree without damaging them? There is a bumper crop and the trunk is thick, so there is no chance of shaking it to loosen them.

What you mustn't do is wait for the pears to drop off of their own accord. If they are left to ripen on the tree, pears become overripe and lose their texture, turning brown in the middle. They are best picked when they are almost ripe (their skin starts to turn slightly lighter, and the fruits come away easily when given a slight twist), then left to ripen in the fruit bowl for a few days. You will need a fruit picker. These usually combine a blade for cutting the stem with a small basket for catching the fruit. The whole thing is on an extendable arm and operated by pulling a string. Gardena (gardena. co.uk) has a good one with a cotton basket and stainless steel blade that is used with telescopic handles to extend the reach to 4m, and you could stand on a ladder with a trusted friend at the bottom to reach a little higher.

We've got a sticky problem with the railway sleepers that make up a few bits of our garden's infrastructure (steps and so on) – namely, as soon as the sun comes out, they leak tar. With young children toddling around, this has been damaging clothes and getting walked into the house. How can we treat them?

Unfortunately the very common British pine sleepers (from which the British railway system was constructed) are the worst offenders for this. There is no effective way to treat them. Mopping up with sand or sawdust helps in the short-term, but every time the weather warms up the gooey stuff will be on the move again. Because of the fairly recent realisation of just how toxic creosote is, an EU law now prohibits creosote-treated sleepers from being used anywhere they will be in frequent contact with skin, so try to keep the kids away from them. Consider facing the sleepers with wood to cover up the seepage, or even having them replaced: railwaysleeper.com is a good source of advice and supplies many different types.

What to do this week

This weekend is the latest you should even think about pruning hedges, especially evergreen ones. A cut now will allow plants to put on a little growth before the onset of cold weather stops play, leaving them looking crisp yet slightly fuzzy around the edges through winter – surely the look we are all aiming for. Leave it any later, and you risk them being at a stage of soft, vulnerable growth when the cold bites, leading to all manner of horticultural horrors, such as brown patches and bare, twiggy bits.

The timing of your potato harvest is a very tricky business indeed: you want the skins to have toughened up enough to store well, but maturity sends a signal to an army of spud-loving slugs, which always move in at this time. If yours are usually riddled, get them up good and early, when the foliage first starts dying down. Brush off the soil, rinse and give them an afternoon basking in the sun, before packing up the immaculate ones in hessian or paper sacks. Boil or roast the imperfect ones as soon as possible.

Putting your green tomatoes on a sunny windowsill to ripen will just give you unripe tomatoes with extra-tough skin. That's because, once a tomato is off the plant, it prefers a bit of gloom to ripen up in. If you want your crop to ripen quickly, pop them in a paper bag with a banana skin, and put the whole thing in a drawer. For a succession of slow-ripening tomatoes, stack them in an airy crate and store them in a dark place, and skip the banana skin. Check and eat regularly.

Mid September

In my new and previously neglected garden, at least 75 per cent of the 'lawn' is bindweed, dandelions and horsetails. I am averse to using chemicals, but suspect I'll need them. I'm not after a bowling green but I'd like more grass than weeds.

Horsetail and bindweed won't survive regular mowing, and the same will reduce dandelions to a rosette that can be dug up with a trowel. This is definitely the route to take if you don't want to use chemicals. You may need to hire a strimmer to get the whole mess short enough to mow in the first place, but after that it will all come down to regular mowings. Do it once a week for now, until growth slows, and then in spring start cutting furiously at the first signs of growth, at least once a week. Any borders will be harder work, as you won't have this regime to keep weeds down. If you are making any new ones, ensure you dig out every root painstakingly first.

I have a four-year-old lemon tree, in a generous-sized pot, which has survived many winters outdoors (in a fleece). It is big and strong, but has never produced a single lemon, nor a flower for that matter. Where am I going wrong?

Although lemons survive out of doors in milder areas, flowering and subsequent fruiting is dependent on warmth. They will flower all year round given sufficiently high temperatures, but spring is prime time and yours spends every spring recovering from its winter chill. Lemons do best with a winter temperature of between 10C and 20C (overheating in winter can also suppress flowering), so move it into a conservatory or a frost-free greenhouse, or just indoors into a brightly lit but cool spot such as a porch or unheated utility room. Do this now, before the nights get too cold, and keep it inside until the weather has really warmed up in spring. Don't panic if only a tiny fraction of flowers turn into fruit as this is normal. Those that do can take up to 18 months to ripen.

My palm tree looks like it's giving up. The lower leaves are brown and fall out constantly. The upper ones are still green, but how long will it remain alive, as most of the leaves have fallen off? The tree is about 14ft high and the trunk is tripartite. It gets little light. I hope you can help.

I am going to suggest that this is not a palm at all, but a cordyline. These have a palm-like habit and are commonly, and wrongly, known as cabbage palms. There are only a few palms that are hardy enough to survive in the UK, and the most common of these don't have a branching habit. Cordylines produce a rosette of arching, long, thin leaves, while true palms have hand-shaped leaves, or a series of leaflets coming from a central leaf stalk. It is important you know the difference, because cordylines can be pruned back hard and will resprout from the base, whereas if you cut off the top of a palm, it will die. Both palms and cordylines shed lower leaves regularly. This is how they form their trunk. You can just pull them off or cut them off with secateurs. However, it sounds as if yours has got a bit drawn and spindly, probably because it is trying to reach up for the light. If you can positively identify it as a cordyline, cut it back hard and allow it to resprout. Then feed and water it throughout next spring and summer.

On one side of our garden we have a mixed hedge, including service trees and viburnum. Can you just let them grow, or do they need to be pruned? I prefer a wild, left-alone look.

The trouble with leaving hedges 'wild' is that they quickly turn into rows of trees and are then of little use as boundaries. Regularly pruning it into a hedge shape would make it thicken out below, but you could be a bit different and enlist the services of a hedge layer (plants regenerate from the base after being cut almost all the way through then laid at an angle). Old and neglected hedges benefit most, although you can lay a fairly young hedge, too. It's good for wildlife and a part of our heritage and all that, but I'd go for it just because it looks great. The National Hedgelaying Society (hedgelaying.org.uk) lists contractors.

What's the best way to tackle extremely vigorous ground elder that is taking over my shrubs and hedge, and encroaching on my neighbour's garden?

This is a big problem, and the road will be long, fiddly and boring. But it can be done. Start by digging up the rhizomes, which are the source of the brute's strength. However, I am rather concerned about your shrubs, because the elder roots will be all around their roots. By far the best course of action is to dig them all up, clean them off and replant them in pots or in elder-free areas of the garden, which will be a whole lot of fun. After all that, you will still have a problem. It's then a case of either constant weeding or frequent use of a weedkiller, neither of which is guaranteed to work. If you want to go the weedkiller route paint the remaining elder stems this autumn with a glyphosate-based weedkiller. Repeat next summer, once there is plenty of growth, and then continue endlessly.

I have saved seed from a group of Iceland poppies, which have particularly attractive coral-pink flowers, that I found growing in a car park. Will it be sufficient just to scatter them about, or is there a better way to give them a good chance?

Well done for getting started on this now – the plants will be larger and more floriferous from an autumn sowing than if you had waited until spring. There are a couple of things you can do to improve prospects. Start by preparing the ground: break up large pieces of earth with a fork and then a rake, to get as close to a fine, crumbly texture as you can, then sow thinly, in neat rows. This helps when trying to differentiate between seedlings and weedlings. Thin seedlings later in autumn, so they are a few inches apart, and again in spring, to about 30cm apart. Be aware, however, that your seedlings may not have exactly the same colouring as the parent plants.

What to do this week

Hedgehogs, those snuffling garden defenders, will lose up to a third of their body weight during winter hibernation, and they are fattening themselves up in preparation now. Put out cat and dog food, minced meat and scrambled eggs, or buy special hedgehog food, but skip the traditional bread and milk because it upsets their stomachs. A teepee of logs covered with a plastic sheet will provide a welcome home, and if you manage to entice one, it will be raring to gorge itself on your slugs and snails come spring.

The time is ripe for guerrilla gardening action. Seed bombs are little balls of compost, native wildflower seed, clay powder and water, dried, then lobbed on to waste land, abandoned building plots or students' gardens to create heart-lifting beauty among the ugliness. Thrown now, autumn rain will soften the balls and germinate the seeds, making for big, strong plants next summer. Visit guerillagardening.org for more inspiration, and to join the revolution.

As apples ripen, check out how well they were pollinated. To do so, cut one cross-wise – there should be five compartments with two seeds in each. Any fewer than eight seeds altogether indicates a lack of nearby trees that flower at the same time as yours, which means your apples are not the best they could be. Fruit tree nurseries will be able to advise on suitable pollination partners, or look in *RHS Fruit And Vegetable Gardening*, by Michael Pollock (Dorling Kindersley).

Late September

My small patch of lawn suffers from my neighbour's earth-sapping conifers. It is riddled with moss and dandelions and has very poor actual grass. I am constantly being told to dig it up and put down gravel, but I love it and will do whatever it takes to keep it green and healthy. Please help.

You are right to do your best to hang on to it – time-consuming they may be, but lawns are fabulous things. Anyway, it's not much fun lounging on gravel. Conifers generally have shallow root systems, so they are in direct competition with your lawn for surface moisture and nutrients. On the plus side, this means there is some mileage in erecting a barrier in the soil. Dig a ditch as deep as you can (2ft–3ft would be ideal) and sink in an impenetrable barrier such as corrugated plastic along the length before back filling with soil. Then try all the usual lawn treatments – scratch out moss and dead grass with a spring-tined rake, aerate by sticking a fork into the soil and brushing in topsoil, apply a weed and feed treatment and re-seed. Or go all out and take up the grass, dig over and remove the worst of the roots, replenish the depleted soil with new topsoil and lay yourself a brand spanking new lawn.

For 10 years, my peonies bloomed well, but for the past two years they have had no buds or blooms. They look healthy enough. Have two dry springs affected them?

Peonies like moisture, but yours may have been in one spot for too long. Established peony clumps get congested and need revitalising. Now is a good time to dig them up, divide and replant. This will give them time to get a little established before the cold halts them in their tracks. Cut off the stems, then dig up carefully: the roots are easily damaged. Shake off as much soil as you can – if it's still hard to see what you're doing, wash off the rest. Using a sharp knife, divide the plant into pieces with up to five buds and the same number of bulbous roots. Take care not to plant too deep: this can lead to lots of growth and no flowers. The buds should be no more than 5cm below the surface. Plant about a foot apart. Now the hard part: nip out any flower buds next year to make the plants put all their energy into strong root growth – your restraint will reap rewards in the future.

I have leatherjackets in my lawn and have read that the best treatments are the chemicals HCH or carbaryl. What products contain them?

Leatherjackets are the babies of the crane fly, which lay eggs into lawns in August. These hatch within a few weeks, and the larvae feed on the roots of the grass through winter, causing yellow patches and slow growth in spring. Treat now, while the soil is still warm and before they do any damage. The chemicals you mention are very nasty, and there is a far more widely used biological alternative – nematodes that eat the grubs. They're mixed with water in a watering can or using a hose-end feeder, and applied to a pre-watered lawn. From greengardener.co.uk.

Is there any way of keeping squirrels off our pear tree? Last year they ate the whole crop before it ripened.

Squirrels are sneaky little critters, and very adaptable. They will find ways around, or simply get used to, most of the controls that are available. The most straightforward way of keeping them off is to buy a fruit cage to cover the entire tree. This is fine if it's a dwarf, but not so practical on larger specimens. You can also try high-frequency sound emitters, though squirrels get used to these, too. I have heard that mothballs, hung from stockings in the tree near the heaviest clusters and changed every few weeks, can be effective. You could also try wrapping some of the fruit in horticultural fleece, or another physical barrier, until it ripens.

My daughter recently came home with a rabbit that likes to eat everything I've planted. Can you recommend any shrubs that it won't eat (apart from rosemary and lavender), and that are also not poisonous?

Not only has your daughter introduced a major pest to your garden, but you now have to replant to avoid poisoning it? The sheer nerve. Rabbits will take a speculative nibble on just about everything but, as you have noticed, they are less keen on strongly smelling plants that are high in oils, such as the silver-leafed Mediterranean shrubs. Of these, you could also try santolina, nepeta and mint. Others to try include holly, fuchsia, box, cornus and buddleia, but bear in mind that new plants will be both more vulnerable and also tempting to your new pet than older, tougher plants, so erect barriers, such as small chicken wire fences, to protect them at first. Or you could buy a rabbit run and go back to planting what you like.

We recently pulled down an ivy that grew through a large wild cherry tree, and there are now no leaves on the tree's lower branches. Can we cut it back to stimulate new growth? We are in a conservation area, but I believe we are allowed to pollard.

Hold it right there. Don't even think about doing a single thing to a tree in a conservation area without seeking permission first. But before doing that, you need to work out just what it is you want to do – and it certainly isn't pollarding. Cutting back, as you might a lanky bedding fuchsia, won't work, although it may produce 'water shoots': that is, thin, straight stress growths that are no good to anyone. And do nothing for a while, anyway, because the tree may just recover by itself. Give it a few treats – an autumn mulch of composted leaves, a spring feed, water and mulch – to increase its chances. If you find you need to remove the dead lower branches, call in a qualified arborist and fill out all the necessary forms.

What to do this week

If you have trees overhanging your garden pond, throw a length of pea netting, or similar, over it now, before the leaves start falling. This simple act will save you from having to fish them out later with a net. If you've never done either – the netting or the net – I'll bet you've got a problem with blanket weed. A build-up of rotting debris at the bottom of a pond is one of the things that causes such troublesome algae in the first place, so prevention now should mean clearer water and less work next summer.

Back in the bad old days, every dead stem of every perennial plant was stripped to the ground in the big autumn tidy-up. Nowadays we tend to leave them be until spring, enjoying their winter skeletons and allowing wildlife to benefit from the seed heads and the extra cover. However, some things still need pruning, namely roses and fruit. Rose bushes should be reduced in height by about a third, to prevent wind rock. Apple and pear pruning will come a bit later, in December.

Sales of spring bulbs are apparently soaring, but alliums are the bulb of the moment, says David Saunderson of bulb supplier de Jager (dejager.co.uk), particularly the vibrant A. 'Purple Sensation'. Plant them throughout your border now and their lollipop heads will rise above the surrounding planting in early summer.

End of September / beginning of October

I would like to plant a quince tree in my south-facing garden which gets lots of sun, fairly high winds and is very near the sea in the east of Scotland. Would it survive and which variety would be best?

This is a far from ideal spot for a quince. They are hardy, but they like a sheltered spot in order to crop well. Generally they are thought to struggle north of Yorkshire, but they are grown in Scotland and it is worth a go, particularly with a really hardy variety such as 'Leskovac' (from Larch Cottage Nurseries in Cumbria, larchcottage.co.uk). One of the problems with growing fruit trees in windy conditions is that bees and other pollinators cannot linger long enough to do their work, so the tree might grow OK but without producing much fruit. If you could protect it from the wind, perhaps with shelter from a hedge or other planting, you would have much more luck.

I have a birch sapling on my lawn. There's space for it to grow a natural canopy, but I want it to grow in width, not height. Can I coppice it?

Coppicing is the practice of cutting a tree's shoots down to the ground before letting it reshoot. This was originally carried out in managed woodlands to create a renewable source of wood. Traditionally, birch is coppiced every few years, which keeps it pretty small, but since you have the space, it might be better to coppice it just the once, so creating a multistemmed tree. This will give you the lower, wider shape you want, while at the same time giving the bark time to develop its full colour and the stems to form a good shape. Coppicing should be started when the tree is as young as possible, so your sapling is probably at the perfect age. Most coppicing is carried out in spring, so the tree can then burst into growth and quickly recover. But birch is a little different in that it can bleed sap from any pruning cuts, so pruning should be carried out between midsummer and autumn, when the sap is not rising.

My blackcurrant bush was laden with berries this summer, but most fell off rotten without ripening. What might be causing this?

When fruits seem to form well but then drop before they reach maturity, the answer usually lies with the flowers, so the problem is likely to have occurred much earlier in the year than you might imagine, when the flowers were being pollinated. It's possible that your bush was hit by a late frost, so if your area is prone to them, protect the bush with fleece at next year's flowering time. To avoid the problem altogether, those in cooler areas should ideally plant a late-flowering type such as 'Ben Sarek' or 'Ben Tirran'. There is also a chance that your problem is due to your bush not getting enough water this spring. Next year, make sure it is well watered at flowering time.

My terraced house faces north and gets no sun. There is about 1m of concrete between the house and the pavement. Is there anything I can grow in the cracks?

Your choices are limited, but you are right to try, because bare, cracked concrete is far from the best welcome home. Mentha requienii, Corsican mint, and penny royal, M. pulegium, (from chilternseeds.co.uk), both have tiny leaves that creep along cracks and give off fresh, minty wafts when walked on. In my own shady cracks, I have the controversial Soleirolia soleirolii, or mind-your-own-business. It makes a lovely fresh green creeper, but plant it only where there is no danger of it escaping into the larger garden, or it'll be there for life. Mix seeds (in the case of the mints) or small bits of chopped up leaf and stem (the soleirolia) into compost, pour into the cracks, and keep moist.

I have dormant bulbs in various places in a border that is covered in weeds. In the past, I hand-weeded, but I am now over 80 and find it a chore. No one can tell me of a weedkiller suitable for use over bulbs. Can you help?

The chemical you are looking for is glyphosate which, it is claimed, breaks down on contact with the soil. Although it has always been marketed as an environmentally-sound chemical that does not harm soil organisms or get into ground water (it has even been accepted for use in organic systems in some parts of the world), it is worth mentioning that serious doubts have been raised about its toxicity to both humans and the environment, and great controversy now surrounds any environmental claims. Glyphosate won't harm your bulbs, however, as long as you use it only when they are completely dormant. For the future, why not consider planting some ground-cover plants, such as geraniums, which will suppress the weeds, but which the bulb foliage can grow through?

We stripped 30 years of ivy growth off the walls of our house, but it has left marks and the remnants of tiny tendrils, which no amount of wire brushing can shift. How can we remove them before we repaint the walls?

I get many, many questions about this and I have avoided them until now, as 'Abandon all hope!' doesn't make for a very enlightening answer. But the clamour has become deafening, so I will tell you what I know. A wire brush, paint scraper or pressure washer just won't do it. You are wasting your time and damaging your walls. It is all about time and patience. If you can live with the damage for a few years, those tenacious little blighters just may have shrivelled and rotted slightly, enough finally to succumb to the attentions of a firmly wielded wire brush. Painting over them now will not only look rubbish but will also seal them in for eternity, so resist, and settle in for the long haul.

What to do this week

Some herbs that die down outdoors in autumn will keep on producing if dug up and moved inside for winter. Treat yourself to some smart little terracotta pots with trays, then lift, divide and plant up chives, mint, parsley and oregano. Give them a week or so in a shady spot outdoors to get used to lower light levels, then pop them on a windowsill for fresh leaves even on the darkest days.

If you have a big bulb order arriving, or if you are planning any autumn or winter planting, take time to mark the locations of your perennials now as they die down (and those of any existing clumps of bulbs, if you can remember that far back). Use plant labels, sticks or even tent pegs. You don't need to know what they are, just where, otherwise you risk digging up old favourites in your giddy haste to squeeze in the newcomers.

Fallen half-fermented apples litter the ground and act as filling stations for drunken, aggressive wasps. Unappealing as this half-brown, insect-bitten bounty looks, if you want to put it to a more useful purpose, pop it into a series of small plastic bags and put them in the freezer. Then, in the depths of winter, defrost a bag or two and lay on a banquet for birds such as thrushes and blackbirds, which will do just about anything for a bit of half-rotten fruit.

Early October

My allotment is infected with club root, so I won't be planting brassicas. Any suggestions for other vegetables, apart from the obvious peas, fruit, potatoes and beans?

Club root is a fungal disease that hangs about in the soil and causes swellings in the roots of brassicas, leading to stunted growth, yellowing and wilting. There are loads of vegetables other than brassicas, but if you're looking for a replacement winter-cropping, leafy green veg, then try spinach, perpetual spinach and Swiss chard. The best flavoured of these is spinach, and it can still be sown now, under cover, and should produce leaves this winter except during the coolest spells. You could, of course, try a few tricks to outwit the club root. Rotate brassicas to different parts of the allotment each year (ideally, five years should pass before they're grown again in the same piece of ground). Applications of lime to raise the pH and of organic matter to improve drainage can also help. Club root attacks usually happen on the delicate new root systems of direct-sown seedlings, so sow your own seedlings in pots or buy them in, and then plant them straight into their final positions. Good sources of seedling vegetable plants are Delfland Nurseries (organicplants.co.uk) and Marshalls Seeds (marshalls-seeds.co.uk).

Last year, I planted a mixed beech, hawthorn and privet hedge. Now my neighbour has planted three willows just 1ft away. I am watering daily. Am I fighting a losing battle?

What a mean neighbour! Willows (Salix alba var. vitellina) are moisture sappers, so your hedge might suffer in the long run, but at least you have a year's start on the willows. You need to get your hedge established, so that it can compete. Daily watering is OK, but the ground really needs a good soaking, so the hedge roots go down deep to access more moisture reserves. Light watering can encourage surface rooting. Run a soaker hose along the hedge, and give less frequent but longer waterings. Better, try to convince your neighbour to coppice or pollard the willows annually. That way, they won't be such a pain for you, and your neighbour will get manageable trees with attractive colourful stems all winter.

I live in a basement rear flat and the steps get slippery and slimy when wet. I don't want to spend £15 on a patio cleaner as I think there is a cheaper way of getting rid of this muck. Any suggestions?

The slimy stuff is algae and it is best removed with a bleach-and-water mix. In fact, according to pavingexpert.com, it pays to be a skinflint when it comes to patio cleaners, as some contain hydrochloric acid, which can damage concrete and some types of stone. Go for the cheapest watery bleach, rather than the thick, toilet-bowl type. Mix it half and half with water, and sprinkle it on with a watering can. Leave for a few minutes, then wash it off. You may have to do this a few times, the first time. After this, repeat at regular intervals.

I have a flourishing shrub rose, known to be at least 75 years old. Is there any method of taking a cutting for a neighbour?

Cuttings are a cheap way of increasing your roses, but work best with old varieties (as opposed to merely elderly ones). Commercially, modern hybrid teas and floribundas are grafted on to vigorous rootstocks, and on their own roots they may be slow-growing, and struggle to root. It is so easy it is worth a try, and autumn is the time to do it. Choose a shoot that has flowered this year and cut a large section of stem, about 30cm long. Remove any remaining leaves from the bottom two-thirds, and cut off the top. Make a trench in a sunny part of the garden and fill it with compost mixed with plenty of sand, vermiculite or perlite for drainage. Dip the cutting in rooting hormone and push the bottom two-thirds into the trench. They should be ready to lift and plant up next autumn.

Some of the brick facings on my garden wall have come off due to moisture and frost. I have repaired them using cement and cement dye, but I am not excited by the results. How can I make them look like the original bricks?

I know nothing of brick repair, but I do know how to harness the magical camouflaging properties of moss to cover up a dodgy repair job. Even the cheapest and most naff concrete garden-centre pot can be made to look like an heirloom once moss-encrusted, and if it is moisture that has done for your old bricks, then you have the perfect moss-growing spot. The usual ageing technique is to paint the item with yogurt and let the life forms find it, but the moss-gardener's trick is to whiz up in a food processor a bit of moss with some buttermilk or beer, and paint that on. Add a spoonful or two of water-retaining gel to help things along.

We want to plant a hedge of pleached trees to hide a neighbour's ugly wall (about 9ft tall). Can you advise on a suitable tree at a reasonable price? Quotes from the garden centre have come in at £1000 per tree.

Pyracanthas in their loose, natural form are not a favourite of mine, but I have recently seen two that were constrictively trained and they looked marvellous. One was turned into a 'cloud' tree, the other grown as an espalier, with branches trained horizontally along evenly spaced wires from one main vertical stem. To get the branches to look tightly trimmed yet covered in berries at this time of year, prune after flowering in midsummer, taking out wayward shoots back to their base and shortening other growths to a few inches. Choose from red ('Red Column'), orange ('Orange Glow') and yellow ('Soleil d'Or'). Colourful, evergreen and dirt cheap.

What to do this week

If your brussels sprouts have grown tall and beautiful, and so are now wafting about in the autumnal breezes, stop them. Roots disturbed by wind rock make for soft, open buttons, rather than the tight, rounded ones you are after. A cane isn't really up to the job – you want to tie them to something stouter, such as a piece of 2x2, pushed firmly into the ground. And remember to hold off eating the little beauties until the first hard frosts, to get them really sweet.

It is cruel and heartless to move an established evergreen, but sometimes you just want to anyway. My bay tree has some important work to do across the garden, blocking a neighbour's new extension, so it's off. October is the month to move it, while the soil is warm and moist yet the sun is no longer beating down and drying out the leaves. First, dig your hole, then dig around and under the poor plant, quickly transferring it. Soak on planting, and whenever it doesn't rain for a while.

You can still sow salad mixes to produce leaves all winter. Thompson & Morgan (seeds.thompson-morgan.com) offers two suitable ones: Niche Oriental Mixed, with red mustard, komatsuna and mizuna, and Niche Blend, with red kale, golden purslane and salad burnet. Sow thinly and chop what you want once it's a couple of inches tall. A sheltered windowbox is perfect but cover with fleece during the harshest weather if in a more exposed position.

Mid October

I give pots good drainage with crocks, perlite and broken polystyrene, but on watering a stream flows from beneath. Should I give up on crocks?

Keep faith – without good drainage, the holes at the base of a pot get clogged up, with either compost or roots, and the plants become waterlogged. If they are suffering, check that the compost hasn't become resistant to water: when some composts dry out, they're hard to re-wet, and water runs off and down the insides of the pot. Dig down into it to search for dry bits, or soak the pot in a basin of water for 24 hours. If you still find dry bits, shake the soil from around the roots and pot into fresh compost in spring.

I have a beautiful white wisteria that has been on my porch for fifteen years. The porch is falling down and has to be replaced. Can I move the wisteria? If not, can I build without disturbing it?

We are getting round to the time of year when deciduous plants can be moved. You must wait until all the leaves have fallen off and they are well into their winter dormancy before you attempt it. I imagine this plant is pretty big, so you will have to prune it to move it. Luckily, wisterias respond well to quite hard pruning, so you can take it down to about 6ft without a problem. Water well before lifting and take as much soil and as many of the tiny fibrous roots as you can. Replant immediately and keep well watered for all of next year. You might find that simply by pruning it, and completing the building over winter, you can leave it where it is.

During recent bad weather, a branch from a neighbour's juniper tree fell off and damaged the house. The rest of the tree looks fine, but now I am worried. What sort of age do junipers reach, and when does their structural integrity become an issue?

You've picked on a real old-timer here – in the US there are junipers that are more than 2,000 years old. That is not to say that your neighbour's tree is going to hang around that long, but it is unlikely to be reaching the natural end of its life any time soon. However, problems with limb drop are not really down to a tree's age, but to its condition, and you are right to be concerned. An arboriculturist will be able to assess the tree and look for danger signs such as limbs at awkward angles, rain pools forming within branch junctures and rotting wood. I strongly advise you to call one in as soon as possible.

I use toilet roll and kitchen roll tubes as biodegradable plant pots for my seedlings. However, the outsides of the 'pots' have become covered in small mushrooms. They are white and grey with stripy caps. Can you tell me what they are and whether they will damage the seedlings?

Despite your detailed description, I am not even going to attempt to work out what these mushrooms are. I can advise you not to eat them, but that's about it. Your seedlings, though, are perfectly safe: the fungus is obviously feeding on the cardboard tubes. Something is biodegradable only if it can become prey to a biological organism, in this case a fungus. You are seeing the fruiting bodies, and the fungus will work perfectly well without them, so break them off if they bother you. I would be concerned only if you noticed any adverse effect on the seedlings. If you do, carry on with your admirable bit of recycling, but cut or slide the tubes off before planting.

I have a Clematis armandii growing over a pergola whose base is devoid of foliage. Can you suggest a climber to hide this? I would prefer flowers, but the clematis casts quite a lot of shade.

You don't think of roses for shade, but several do well as long as they get some sun each day. You do need to pick a bumper flower producer, as some bloom will be sacrificed. 'Golden Showers' is a compact climber that produces bright yellow flowers that leap out from the shade. A very different effect would be produced by 'Ballerina', with its huge heads of tiny white and pink, musk-scented flowers. Both are shade-tolerant and will not grow too large, but strict training and pruning will be required to prevent them going the way of the clematis. Train stems into a fan shape. Prune out the oldest stems each winter and shorten the side shoots to just a few inches.

Our compost bin lid is always covered with worms. I lovingly move them back down the heap to work for me, but wonder if they are up there for a purpose, possibly to breed, because several are entwined and there are lots of baby worms. What is happening, and how should I respond?

Ah, you do conjure a blissful scene. However, they are most probably climbing because the bin is too wet and not, unfortunately, because they have heard that the lid is the spot for hot love action. They are trying to escape drowning and you are 'lovingly' sending them back down to a composty grave. Perhaps you have put in lots of grass clippings and soggy green waste, but little that's woody or papery. Have a feel, and if it is soggy, add some torn-up newspaper to dry it out. Alternatively, they might just have been climbing to cooler spots because they got too warm, and will move back down as the temperature drops. Not as stupid as they look, are they?

My five-year-old lavender has outgrown its space. I want to move it to my friend's front garden where it will have more room. How and when should we do it and how successful will it be?

Any other evergreen and I would tell you to set about it immediately. But lavender is often described as 'short-lived', and after about six years is past its best. They can and do go on longer, but people get sick of them for the exact reason you want rid of yours: they get big and leggy, and they start opening up and show gaping sections of stem. It seems a bit much to foist this fading plant on to your friend just because she is less fussy than you – it's a little like passing on an elderly cat when it starts pooing on the carpet. Dig it up, but put it out of its misery. Help any new plant defy the ageing process by lightly pruning it all over every year, after flowering.

What to do this week

The time has come to get your neglected perennials in order. If any haven't flowered well this year, they are getting old and congested, and need revitalising. Dig them up and split them, using a sharp spade, secateurs or even – if you have been very, very naughty and left them so long they are hard to split – a saw. Mix some compost into their new home, plant, water and forget about them again.

Many apples store well, so don't look on the harvest as a glut. Wrapping will keep them in peak, just-harvested condition. Choose the most perfect, slightly under-ripe ones (no windfalls, they really should be used now), pack into small plastic bags and pierce once. This may sound like a recipe for a bag of mould, but as long as they're stored somewhere evenly cool, such as a shady shed or cellar, condensation will not form and the plastic will prevent shrivelling.

Look at your autumn garden from an insect's-eye view. If it seems bare and lacking in flowers, your resident critters are suffering. Late-flowering plants are visited by honey bees about to go into hibernation and by butterflies to store up strength for autumn migrations, so consider planting to help them out in future years. Asters, echinaceas, solidago, sedum, eupatorium, liatris and agastache are all high in nectar and will act as an essential last-stop insect shop. They're mighty pretty, too.

Late October

Two years ago, a gardener friend pruned my apple trees severely. The foliage has grown back well, but no fruit has developed. How long will the trees take to crop again?

They are friend or gardener, certainly not both. Fruit trees crop best on old wood, as your 'friend' would have known had they looked into the matter before making merry with the pruning saw. New trees take between three and five years to start cropping, so this may be a rough guide to how long your sproutings will take to bear fruit. However, consider replacing the trees if they are getting on a bit. Quantity and quality of fruit decline as trees age, and it is going to be a struggle to get them back into good cropping order. If you do decide to keep them, carry out renovation pruning over the winter. Select about five shoots per tree to be your main stems. They should be well spaced and create an open cup shape. All other growth must be removed right back to its point of origin. Don't do all of this at once. You will stress the tree and produce thin, sappy growths that will never amount to anything. Spread your renovation pruning over three years, taking out a third of the unwanted growth each time. Then cut back your main branches by a third, to encourage side shoots to grow the following year. These should be pruned to leave around five buds on each.

My beech hedge is 7ft tall, and as I get older I am finding it increasingly difficult to prune the top. If it were trimmed by 18 inches, would the top eventually become re-leafed?

Yes, a beech hedge will put up with all manner of chopping about and still come back leafy and lovely. Other hedging plants that will tolerate hard pruning are box, yew, laurel, holly and privet. Conifers, other than yew, will not. Cut back deciduous ones over winter, while the leaves are off, and evergreens in early spring (taking care not to disturb any nests). Cut a few inches lower than the height you eventually want, to allow the fresh stuff space to grow. Give the whole length of the hedge a good feed, and water and mulch in spring to help it recover.

Sadly, we have just removed a large robinia tree that was planted about 3m away from our kitchen window (at the limit of our front garden) to block out a neighbouring ugly garage wall. Can you suggest an alternative small tree?

I can't imagine the robinia was doing much of a job of hiding the wall – just a thin strip of it behind the trunk, surely? A shrub might be more the thing for such blocking intentions and they can be made to look awfully tree-like with judicious pruning. Hamamelis (or witch hazel) might fill the space perfectly, and if you go for 'Jelena' or 'Diane', it will give you autumn colour as well as winter flowers. Crab apples are handsome and compact, with lovely, bushy growth to cover the wall, blossoms in spring and fruit in winter to distract you from that annoying view.

My small, six-year-old wildlife pond contains frogs, newts, dragonflies, freshwater snails, oxygenating weeds and water lilies. My brother says it needs cleaning each winter. Is this correct?

Most certainly not – every time you clean your pond, you are wiping out legions of wildlife lovelies, so the less often, the better. Every five years or so it becomes necessary, perhaps as it silts up, if the pond liner needs repairing, or when plants need splitting. For fish ponds, late spring is the right moment, but for a wildlife pond autumn is better. Remove at least some of the water, and transfer all snails, newts, frogs and plants to a tank filled with the old water. Then pile up dead plant growth by the side of the pond, to be thrown away after a few days – this gives creatures living in it time to crawl out and back into the pond. Remove the silt but keep a bucketful aside to put back in later, because this, too, will be teeming with life.

Clean and repair the pond liner, then split plants and re-plant, before refilling with water.

Our redcurrant bushes had a good crop this year, but they have developed a greyish-green fungus on their branches. How can I treat this? There seems to be some on nearby apple trees, too.

This sounds more like lichens, which live on plants but don't harm them. However, it is not all good news. They are more likely to alight on slow-growing plants, so this may be a sign that both apples and redcurrants are diseased or struggling. They may just need a boost, so redouble your efforts with respect to mulching and feeding in spring. But plant growth will slow as plants age. Redcurrants start to decline after 10–15 years. Apple trees can go on far longer, but they, too, will decline and eventually fade away. You will most probably get several more good years out of them, but plant replacements now, so they're ready to step into the breach when the moment comes.

I seem to be unlucky (or inept) with mint and lemon balm. The mint especially looks sickly and discoloured, with rust-coloured spots underneath the leaves, which then take over the whole leaf. I have started with new plants but the same has happened again.

This is mint rust, which also affects lemon balm. The plants soldier on for a while looking pallid and unappetising, but the disease will eventually kill them. You can attempt to get rid of bad infestations using heat: place some straw on the top of the foliage and burn the lot (not suitable for those in plastic pots). With new plants, provide perfect conditions so they are not stressed: both like partial shade and a moist, but not waterlogged, soil, so in a pot use drainage crocks and a moisture-retentive compost such as John Innes No 3.

Mints grown in containers should be removed, chopped into quarters and re-potted every spring, or the vigorous roots will get choked up. Feed twice a year with a balanced fertiliser. Keep a lookout for the telltale red spots under the leaves, and remove and burn them as soon as you see them.

What to do this week

If we've escaped frost till now, it isn't far off. Remove pumps from ponds, drain out and store hosepipes, and wrap or drain outdoor taps. And don't forget the plants. Even some of those we call hardy prefer a little winter comfort. Gunnera crowns should be blanketed with their old leaves, and a thick dry mulch of straw or conifer boughs (it's all they're good for, if you ask me) placed over the crowns of delicate perennials such as penstemon and agapanthus.

Placing grease bands around the trunks of fruit trees is the type of proper gardening your grandad would be proud of. The grease – in what must surely be a comedy fashion – prevents the wingless female winter moth from climbing the tree to lay her eggs from November to January. The resulting caterpillars lay waste to leaves in spring and early summer, weakening trees and ushering in disease. Glue bands stop them too, but are not so funny. Neither has any effect on the winged females of the dastardly codling moth, the maggot of which turns up alarmingly in the centre of the apple.

There is no great rush to plant tulips – they get a bit previous if the soil is still warm, so November planting is perfect. You should, however, begin choosing and ordering. Tulipa 'Ballerina' is a lovely choice: elegant, lily-flowered blooms in dodgy-boiler-flame orange and with a nice scent, too. So, if visitors stifle gasps and whisper about your lack of tulips next spring, don't say you weren't told.

End of October / beginning of November

I have a young apple tree that has produced fine fruit at the top but miserable specimens further down. Is there a reason for this?

Most fruit formation problems date back to blossom time. If your tree is planted in a dip or at the bottom of a hill, it may be in a frost pocket. On calm, clear, cold nights, frost pours downhill and gathers in such pockets, and it is then that you get blossom damage (and later fruit damage) from the bottom up. Check the lie of the land to see if there is anything you can do to prevent frost from pooling, such as cutting a gap in a hedge to allow it to drain away. Alternatively, protect your tree with fleece when it is flowering, although this is only practical while it is still small.

My garden is surrounded by plane and oak trees, so is always in full or partial shade. I would like to grow flowers and some interesting ferns. Currently, teasels, cardoons and nettles thrive.

There is no point in fighting this: you'll have to make it a woodland garden. This should at least make the planning a little easier, as you can choose from a group of plants that will look natural together. The problem with trees is they cast dry shade, which is far tougher on plants than moist shade, but you can improve their chances by finding pockets of soil between the roots and digging in compost before planting. The mainstay of any garden under trees has to be bulbs. They have evolved their life cycle to fit around that of the trees, so leap into life in early spring, flower, absorb sunlight and moisture, and disappear back under the ground before the trees have even produced their leaves. Fill the garden with snowdrops, scillas, wood anemones (A. nemorosa) and bluebells. Suitable shrubs include dogwoods, witch hazels, holly and snowberry. There are lots of perennials to choose from, including hostas, hellebores, foxgloves, violas, tiarella, euphorbia and certain geraniums, such as G. macrorrhizum. Two good ferns for dry shade are Athyrium niponicum var. pictum (the Japanese painted fern) and Polystichum acrostichoides.

This year, I tried to grow strawberries in hanging baskets. Fruit was almost non-existent, although the plants flourished. Tomatoes, grown similarly alongside, produced the usual bumper crop. Where did I go wrong?

If you planted them in spring, they will not have had enough time to get roots established before flowering and fruiting began. The tomatoes are annuals, and are supposed to do their thing in one season, but strawberries take a little longer. The good news is that they grew well, so they should prove less disappointing next year. If you try this again, plant runners in autumn, rather than spring, and then you will get a good crop in summer. By the way, don't mollycoddle them over winter – they need to get a bit of a chill for a really good crop.

What do you recommend to get rid of liverwort? We have it growing in the cracks between paving and on the surface of plant pots. We would prefer a non-toxic solution.

Liverwort thrives only in damp, poorly drained areas, so anything you can do to increase drainage will help. With your pots, this should be fairly straightforward – next spring when repotting, shake the compost from around the roots and replant into a mixture of compost and grit, placing broken crocks in the base to ease the flow of water. You could also try dabbing it with vinegar, which is said to kill it.

We have recently moved to north Wales and would like to grow an orchard with local varieties of fruit, but do not know where to start. We have heard there is a Denbigh plum. Do you know where we can buy it?

In a tricky climate such as that of north Wales, it is not just romantic to grow local varieties. The wetter climate besets traditional English varieties with fungal problems, and you need trees that have proved themselves over many years, particularly if you plan to do without fungicides and grow organically. Ian Sturrock & Sons supplies a number of rare Welsh trees, including the apple 'Anglesey Pig's Snout' (a cooking apple grown on Anglesey since the 1600s), the pear 'Snowdon Queen' (discovered in former gardens on the slopes of Snowdon, and one of the few pears not to suffer cracked fruit in wet climates) and 'Denbigh Plum' (sweet and juicy, it has been around since 1785). Visit iansturrockandsons.co.uk for more.

Three years ago, I bought a bottlebrush plant cutting at an open garden visit. I put it in a pot and placed it in a sunny position, and in winter I wrap it up in an unheated greenhouse. For some reason it has never flowered and now looks straggly.

Callistemons are the ultimate weird and wonderful Aussie plant, the horticultural equivalent of the platypus. Because of their provenance, many think they thrive in dry conditions, when in fact they prefer moister soils. I suspect you may be letting it get a bit dry, as is the tendency in pots – repot it into a larger container, and increase watering. Don't start feeding it now – you'll be wasting your time for this year – but next summer feed regularly. Without knowing what bottlebrush you've got exactly, it is hard to know how hardy it is, but that said your provision of extra winter protection is spot on. Bottlebrushes do toughen up as they get older, and you may get away with leaving yours outside and just wrapping it in fleece this winter. Prune the moment after flowers fade – when you eventually get some.

What to do this week

Greenhouses can be made relatively cosy for winter even if you don't have a power supply or heater. Wash off any remaining shade paint and buy a big roll of bubble wrap before stapling or clipping this to the frame. Smaller enclosures within this, such as a homemade bubble wrap tent, will keep your most precious ones out of the worst frosts. Make sure you can still open windows on warm days, otherwise it could all get a bit sweaty and unhygienic.

It is tempting on a crisp autumn day to have a bonfire to tidy up all the prunings and dead bits of the garden, but it is not very environmentally friendly and your neighbours (at least those who have no romance in their souls) may object to the smell. Instead, make a log pile. There is no more to this than piling up logs and clippings and leaving them to rot down, but it will attract frogs, toads, newts, centipedes (all good slug eaters), beetles and fungi.

If you haven't yet tucked up your exotics for winter, time is running out. Suffolk Herbs (suffolkherbs.com) has a range of Easy Fleece Jackets to keep tree ferns, palms and young cordylines snug. They just slide over plants and pull closed with a drawstring. Hardy bananas need more Heath Robinson-esque protection, such as an enclosure of chicken wire stuffed with straw, while gingers in the ground should be covered with a straw mulch.

Early November

I have three olive trees (which produced full-size fruits this year) growing in identical, dark grey metal containers. At the base of the trees is barren, exposed soil. What can I plant to complement them and give year-round interest?

To really complement olive trees, look to the garrigue, the low-growing Mediterranean habitat that surrounds so many old olive plantations and, happily, from which so many of our best garden plants hail. If your olives are doing this well you must be providing a well-drained soil and plenty of sunshine, and these conditions will also suit garrigue-dwellers such as lavender, rosemary, artemisia, cistus and thyme. They will provide silvery evergreen foliage, early summer flowers and the astringent aromas of the Mediterranean scrub. I can almost hear the cicadas.

I have two very unsightly downpipes at the back of my house. I have tried to grow climbers up them, but because I can grow only in containers, the plants do not reach the tops of the pipes. Is there any product out there that can be attached to the downpipes, and in so doing hide them and make them look more appealing?

Such a thing does exist, but I am not sure about the logic. Surely the eye doesn't normally register downpipes, dustbins, drains, telephone lines and other necessities – they are just part of the furniture. By attaching something to your pipes, you may simply be drawing attention to them – in which case you may be better off painting them a colour close to that of the house, or even just a colour that you like. If you are determined to festoon the pipes with plants, though, you could do worse than have a look at spanishrings. com, which supplies the rings that hold up the terracotta pots that fill Spanish walls and courtyards with flowers. I'm not sure about the authenticity of the one for drainpipes, but it will do the trick.

After my Aeonium aboreum was blown over, I potted up the rosettes that had snapped off. They have all rooted and are thriving, but are all still single-stemmed, like big, top-heavy lollipops. Is there any way I can make them branch?

I'm afraid you just have to lop off the tops. Take a good couple of inches of stem with it, and then you can make this into a cutting, too. It is best to leave the cutting to dry out for a couple of days before potting on, but you know that already. Stem-forming aeoniums tend to branch more when they are well fed and growing strongly, so make sure yours are in adequately sized pots and getting regular water and feed. They can be watered surprisingly often in summer: soak them once a week and feed once a month.

Our walnut tree has looked distressed for a few years now. New shoots stay like spikes, and where leaves do come out, some are curly. It bore only a couple of nuts this year. It was last pruned three years ago.

The pruning most probably started this. Walnuts hate it, and sulk, and opportunistic diseases are always on the look-out for stressed trees with big, open wounds. Pete Wignall, owner of the Grafted Walnut Company (graftedwalnuts.co.uk), suggests two possible diseases. Walnut blight produces dark, angular blotches on the leaves and die-back of stems; leaf blotch produces brown blotches on the leaves, and can make young nuts blacken and drop. There is no cure for either, but you can improve health and prospects. Rake up and burn all of the affected leaves before the new leaves emerge, and try a spray of a copper fungicide such as Bordeaux mixture just before bud break. Wignall waters in a seaweed feed before and after bud break, and sprays it on the leaves in midsummer.

My garden is infested with horsetail. I have tried everything: digging, hoeing, even the dreaded Roundup, despite wanting to be green. I have arthritis and the garden is getting wild and out of control – I have been told to concrete over the lot.

A big part of organic gardening is acceptance. Yes, it is a huge job to get rid of horsetail, but you can rub along with it. I know, because I have it in my own garden. I just chop it off when I see it and then forget about it. Yours can be brought under control with regular, repeated hoeing. Ask a local gardener to give you a quote for a tidy-up of all the weeds and undergrowth, and to lay a lawn. Horsetail grows through lawns but doesn't survive repeated mowing, and it's much more eco-friendly than concrete (lawns kept free of weedkiller provide an excellent habitat for insects; concrete not only means those creatures lose a home, but its production is responsible for at least 5 per cent of the world's CO_2 emissions). Next spring, get some regular help, say every two weeks, to hoe the weeds and mow the lawn. If you can't afford a gardener, contact your local Age Concern group – they sometimes organise volunteers for this sort of maintenance work – or your local volunteer bureau.

I have several old fig trees next to the house wall. Are the roots likely to damage the foundations?

Fig tree roots are extremely strong and have been known to cause damage to pipework and foundations. The fact that your trees are old is in their favour, particularly if they do not appear to have done any damage so far – but keep them pruned so they don't get any bigger. It is always a good idea when planting new figs to restrict their roots, either by planting in a pot and sinking this into the ground, or by creating a sunken box of paving slabs to plant into. This will also improve fruiting.

What to do this week

Why do so many of us use imported bamboo to support our beans, rather than native hazel rods? That is the central question behind Allotment Forestry, an organisation challenging gardeners and allotmenters to plant and coppice their own micro-woodlands, not just for the wildlife benefits, but to make fences, plant supports and fuel. And now is the perfect time to plant your hazel. Each plant will produce 10 long, sturdy poles every five to six years, and will grow beautifully in that tricky, shady corner. Visit allotmentforestry.com for more information.

Pots are in peril. Pots of water-filled soil can freeze solid, expand and crack – and the wind can topple anything top-heavy. They are best grouped together, where they will support each other and provide a little protection for those on the inside, like penguins in an Antarctic storm. Pot feet will lift them above the patio surface and allow unnecessary water to drain away more freely. Particularly precious containers should be given a bubble wrap blanket, just in case.

Peach leaf curl isn't fatal, but it blisters and disfigures to such an extent that plants become weakened. If your peach, apricot or almond tree has been affected, leaf fall is the moment to treat it. The fungal spores overwinter on the tree, and a blast of an organic fungicide such as Bordeaux mixture now may kill them off. Wall-trained trees and little ones in pots should then be covered in plastic to protect against rain, and the whole tree should be treated again in January or February before bud burst.

Mid November

For two years, the shoots on my 'Lord Derby' apple have lost sheen, curled back on themselves and withered. The apples shrivel and the bark splits. Spraying with fungicide slows it, but I can no longer find Benlate.

The RHS advisory service tells me 'Lord Derby' is especially susceptible to blossom wilt, a fungal disease that kicks in about two weeks after flowering. Cut out and destroy all infected parts, not just the withered mini fruits, but all dead twigs and split branches. If left, the fungus forms pustules on the dead bark over winter, which produce spores in spring. Benlate has been withdrawn, but you could try Bordeaux mixture just before bud burst. But don't apply once the flowers are open, as it might harm visiting bees.

We have a tarmac games court. While we are happy that it is shaded in summer, it is unfortunately prone to moss. This makes our geriatric tennis games more like ice hockey. Any suggestions to prevent or remove this menace?

As you suspect, those cooling, shady conditions are causing the problem. You may find that a spanking new covering of tarmac would be less prone to moss, at least for the first few years, and there are moss-killing treatments based on ferrous sulphate available from garden centres. But the trouble with moss is that, if conditions are right, it will always grow back. If the shade is caused by trees, prune them slightly to allow a little light and more air movement, while still retaining some shade. Otherwise, it is down to pressure washing whenever it gets bad. Twice a year should do it.

Our large shed is well covered by climbers, but the roof is covered with roofing felt. I'd like to cover it with wooden roof tiles, which are widely used in Austria, or create a grass or moss roof. Any suggestions?

Those wooden tiles sound wonderful, but I want to nudge you in the direction of a green roof. Not only are they beautiful, but they have a mitigating effect on local flooding, absorbing and gradually releasing rainwater much as soil does, rather than creating the instant run-off of roofs (no matter how attractive). There is too much to green roof construction to go into detail here, but you basically need a waterproofing layer, drainage, planting substrate and plants, all held in place by a wooden frame. Go to livingroofs.org for some examples.

Our grey stone cottage in Dartmoor is surrounded by a concrete path that goes right up to the walls. What could we possibly grow in a large pot (its dimensions are nearly 1m square) in a gloomy spot that gets no direct sunlight?

With all that grey stone and concrete, you must be in dire need of some colour. And, with that in mind, you may want to consider hydrangeas – and if anyone out there thinks they're naff and bourgeois, they are dreadfully behind the times: hydrangeas are, in fact, the new dahlias, fighting their way out of the suburbs with their voluptuous blooms and ability to flower their hearts out in shade. For your (presumably) gusty spot, I'd go for something such as Hydrangea 'Endless Summer' – this is a particularly tough recent introduction that blooms on new growth, so you will get flowers all summer long, even if the old stems are nipped by frost. The flowers can be pink or blue, depending on your soil pH. For a stockist, try ashwood-nurseries.co.uk.

I have a five-year-old acer that I would like to move. When would be the best time to do this?

Anything deciduous can be moved as soon as its leaves have dropped. You then have until spring and the start of new growth, after which you should not try to move it. That said, the earlier you change its position the better, because the soil will still be warm, which will encourage some root growth. This, in turn, will mean the plant is better able to support itself come spring. First, dig the hole into which the plant is to be moved, then dig up the plant, taking a large root ball and as much existing root as possible.

When I came to clear the dead leaves from my pond, I found a spike of bamboo had grown through the side of the pond liner. Major horror! Do I have to dig it up to contain it?

First, you need to know your 'runners' from your 'clumpers'. All bamboos spread by rhizomes (underground stems), but they are divided into two groups depending on how said rhizomes behave. Those of clumpers are small and stocky, so these plants slowly form, er, clumps. Runners' rhizomes can race along for several metres before they send up a shoot. These are the invasive ones, and this is what you've got. Unfortunately, this is what almost everyone's got, as some of the hardiest and most common bamboos – Sasa, Phyllostachys, Pleioblastus, Semiarundinaria – are runners. Suitable clumpers include Chusquea, Yushania and Fargesia. You can contain runners with a solid barrier, such as corrugated metal or plastic. Bury it at least 1m deep, as rhizomes can ricochet off in any direction (including down) when they hit something solid. A simpler solution is to dig a trench of about a spade's depth and width around the plant. Fill this with leaves or twigs. Check the trench every autumn and cut out any rhizomes trying to breach the gap. Either solution involves digging, and the offending escapees will also need digging out. If you are not up to this, throw a few crumbs towards your local landscape gardener, for whom the pickings will be pretty slim at this time of year.

What to do this week

From this removed vantage point, you might feel slightly indulgent towards snails (those pretty shells, those hilarious slimy hermaphrodite sex sessions). Don't be a fool. Catch them unawares as they hibernate in empty pots and under stones. You could turn them out for the birds, but this is the time of year when they are at their tastiest, when snail farmers get their finest harvest and chefs start mixing up garlic butter. Either way, act now and save yourself heartache next spring.

Autumn shouldn't be all about farewells. It can be the best time to get new plants into the ground – perennials as well as bare-root roses, trees and shrubs – so cast your mind back to bare patches and dull spells. If you can't remember any but think the garden looks dreadful now, you need some structure, so major on trees and shrubs. Winter's moisture will allow roots to get a little established before next spring, when any newcomers will romp away in a dazzling fashion.

In milder areas of the country, there is still time to get in a sowing of one of the hardier broad bean varieties such as 'Aquadulce'. The beans will be good and early for harvest – ready around mid-June – but the main advantage of sowing now rather than in spring is that the beans will be well on their way to maturity before the devastating onslaught of blackfly comes around again. To confound the enemy further, pinch out the tips of the plants when the first pods are a few inches long.

Mid to late November

I have two blueberry bushes in pots, and neither of them has fruited this year – one is 75cm high and in a 25cm pot, and was covered in fruit when it was given to me last year and the other bush is smaller, was bought last year and has never fruited.

Blueberry plants take three years from planting to start flowering and fruiting well, so your smaller one is still finding its feet. The larger plant, meanwhile, may have been hit by a late frost (keep some horticultural fleece handy next spring, just in case), but it may also be a problem with pollination. Blueberries fruit best if planted near two companions of different varieties. It may seem daft when you are getting nothing out of your existing bushes, but buying another plant of a different variety should help. All fruit plants do best in the long run if given time to get their roots established before the draining task of fruit production begins. While you're waiting, put them in decent-sized pots (your current pot-to-plant ratio is a little mean), with lots of crocks for drainage. Fill with ericaceous compost and regularly water with rainwater.

I'm interested in growing tea plants and making my own tea. I know it's grown in Cornwall, but don't know where to buy plants or what conditions they need. We have fertile, often damp, clay soil.

A plantation was recently planted in Yorkshire, so tea is not just for the balmy south-west. The tea plant is Camellia sinensis, and if you can grow camellias, you can grow tea (buy plants from the Tregothnan Estate, tregothnan.co.uk). It prefers acidic, moist soil in sun or partial shade (it'll grow in pots of ericaceous compost if your soil is not acidic), and loves dappled shade and lots of leaf mould. Once established, pluck the young leaves every seven to 14 days. Green tea is pretty straightforward to make (steam, then dry the leaves), black tea less so (it involves a fermentation).

I thought we had fruit flies in our kitchen but now wonder if they are fungus gnats. We keep our fruit and veg waste in a small swing-top bin and empty it into the garden compost a few times a week. How can we get rid of these flies/gnats?

Where little flies are near a source of fresh or rotting fruit and vegetables, they are almost certainly fruit flies, not fungus gnats. They are at their worst in late summer and autumn, but can hang around indoor compost bins after outdoor fruits have been harvested and cleared away. The easy answer is to empty your bin more regularly, but that gets less likely as the weather turns nastier. Try a different bin. A swing-top allows flies easy access to the peelings, in which they love to lay their eggs. I use a Compost Caddy (from cat.org.uk/shopping), which is sealed to stop smells escaping and flies entering, and has a replaceable carbon filter to remove odours.

Two years ago, I asked a man to lightly prune my Cheal's weeping cherry tree. Disaster! He reduced it to a stump. It has now reverted to looking much like a common cherry – part of it sad-looking weeping stems, the rest the upright growth of a normal cherry. Can it be saved?

These trees are really two different plants: pieces of a weeping cultivar grafted on to an upright stem. When your man chopped off all your weeping stems, he gave the main stem a chance to send out shoots of its own, and they are now competing with your weeping ones. The answer is simple: chop off the upright shoots, and keep doing it every time they reappear. The tree should then direct all its energy into the weeping stems and they will hopefully start to look healthier. You could also give it a feed and a mulch for a bit of a boost.

One of our borders contains an established snowberry shrub which, despite my best endeavours, seems to become more rampant each year. What is the best way to keep the brute in check, or to get rid of it altogether?

This is a thuggish plant, but pretty, too, particularly in winter when the leaves have fallen and only the pure white berries are left. It will stabilise banks and cover awkward spots, such as among the roots of trees, but it is a bit of a pain in the border. The only way to stop this spread is to be vigilant for the suckers thrown up by the roots. Rather than cutting them off, dig down until you hit the root and then pull away the sucker. If you want to get rid of the whole thing, you can try to dig it out, but it will be back. So, if you're determined to see the back of it, you may have to use something nasty – such as SBK Brushwood Killer – on the stumps and suckers.

Can you give me any tips on how to protect container-based cordylines from strong winds? The wind blows them the wrong way, and they get a gash across the leaf and are permanently creased.

Some people tie the leaves together over winter for this very reason, but it doesn't half look daft and won't help you during summer winds. Protect them the same way you protect anything: with windbreaks. Ideally, a windbreak shouldn't be too solid – wind whips over walls and fences, and then eddies around the base. Trellis is good because it slows wind without blocking it, but twiggy plants are even better. Decide from which direction your prevailing wind blows, and plant shrubs between it and your cordylines. They don't even have to be evergreen – deciduous plants slow wind, too. If the wind whips over the house, plant climbers up the walls. The more planting you have – shrubs, climbers, even trees – the more sheltered you will be, so plant, plant, plant.

What to do this week

Square metres can be lost over the years to creeping grassy paths on the veg patch or allotment. Now that life is a bit calmer on the plot, reclaim some territory. Work out where the boundary of your planted area used to be and stretch some string between two twigs before working along it with a half-moon, if you have one, or a sharp spade. Don't chuck the trimmings on to the compost heap, though, because they'll most probably contain couch grass, which will survive all but the hottest heaps.

Hardwood cuttings are the slow but sure way of propagating deciduous trees and shrubs. Once all the leaves have dropped, cut off a foot or so of growth, then trim away the newer, softer stuff from the tip. Cut 15cm lengths and push into a trench of sandy soil, or put a few around the edge of a pot. Apart from occasional watering, you can then forget about them. Your ranks of willow, dogwood, buddleia, deutzia, hydrangea, virginia creeper, weigela or forsythia will be ready to plant out next autumn.

Forget those run-of-the-mill hyacinths and hippeastrums. For Christmas bulbs that will fill your house brimful with sumptuous springtime scents, try forcing lily of the valley instead. Don't bother digging them up from the garden – you will need to buy these babies in specially. Treated pips will be delivered at the end of November and should then be planted into leaf mould or sand and kept warm, dark and moist until the leaves are 10cm high, when they can be brought out into the light to bloom and whiff. From blomsbulbs.com.

End of November

We have just planted a very large (and expensive) Eriobotrya japonica in a vast container outdoors. By mistake, we used John Innes No2 compost instead of No3. What can we do to redeem the situation, short of repotting, which is not an option?

You're off the hook, actually. Numbers 1, 2 and 3 are made up of exactly the same proportions of loam, peat and sand, but with progressively more nutrients. Your mistake may even work in your favour. Eriobotrya, or loquat, is hardier than its lush, subtropical looks would suggest, but being started into unseasonal growth by an injection of nutrients would make it vulnerable to frost. You will need to pay particular attention to ensuring it is fed regularly when it is in growth. Otherwise, relax.

We have two mature lime trees which last summer suffered badly from aphids, honeydew and a black mouldy residue. Does this harm the plants and the bulbs in the soil below?

Aphids, the honeydew they excrete and the black mould that forms on the honeydew can be worse some years, but will always be present. The only harm to plants below is that they get coated in the honeydew and mould, which can slow growth simply because light struggles to break through. It is not really serious and you can occasionally sponge down badly affected leaves to give the plants a better chance. Bulbs that are under the soil when the aphids are active will not be affected. It is impossible to fully treat trees of this size, but try to get a better balance of aphid and predator in the whole garden. Ladybirds and lacewings are the creatures for the job. Greengardener.co.uk can supply adult ladybirds and lacewing larvae, as well as breeding kits, over-wintering chambers and attractant.

Three months ago, we planted a fremontodendron against an east-facing fence in a clay soil and it has delighted us with lovely yellow flowers. We don't water it much, as I understand it needs very little. But suddenly the leaves have begun to curl and wilt. Can it grow well in our rainy climate?

The most likely explanation is indeed that your conditions are too damp for this Californian native. Root rot is a problem of warm and wet conditions, and often strikes when autumn rains have begun but before the weather has cooled. There is no saving this plant if this is the case, but you could try with a new plant next year. Dig lots of horticultural grit and sand into your clay soil before planting, to improve drainage. Your east-facing wall is perfect, because its shade prevents the soil around the roots from getting too warm while there's enough sun for good flowering. Try a mulch (bark or slate chippings or pebbles) around the plant's base to cool the soil further. Water it in its first year while it's getting established, but do an occasional, deep watering rather than lots of little ones.

This year my phlox, clematis and lilies all failed to flower. I have a small south-facing walled garden and have packed in loads of plants.

There is no problem with putting lots of plants into a confined space, but they will exhaust the soil. Get hold of some well-rotted farmyard manure and mulch the whole bed with it. Repeat this every autumn. Before that, lift the clumps of phlox and lilies, split them a couple of times and replant – congestion is often a cause of blindness in herbaceous perennials and bulbs, and you should do this every few years.

From my first attempt at making compost, I have two bins full. However, loads of little seedlings (possibly tomato) have sprouted. Can I make it usable? And can tomatoes be composted?

Well, the problem is those seeds – they are almost indestructible – they famously crop up around sewage plants. Your compost heap won't have put them through half as much. Spread out the compost in a thinnish layer, leave it for a week or so, then use a hoe to cut down any seedlings that have dared to germinate. However, if you do end up with a few tomatoes in your pots, look on the bright side, you'll be able to make lots of pasta sauce. Next time, however, it may be worth using the 'hot heap' composting method: pay it lots of attention, with frequent shredding and regular turning to get the heat up and keep it that way. Or just miss out the tomatoes altogether.

Our new back garden has a patch of lawn and a few small trees. I'm told that midges are a problem in summer. I'd like to combat them in an environmentally sensitive way.

Midges breed in wet soils. They have become a problem on the west coast of Scotland because of deforestation – trees and woodland understorey take up gallons of water, and without them soils sit soggy. A wet summer will have drenched your garden's soil, and a normal summer (if there is any such thing) might see it midge free. But your new yard sounds as bleak as an overgrazed glen. Plant trees and shrubs to take up excess moisture, and flowering plants to attract predators. Feed the birds and put up bat boxes. The more diverse your garden's habitat, the less likely it is to suffer a midge-blasted fate.

A year ago I pruned my gooseberry bush heavily. This year it has grown well but in some areas it has fruited heavily and in others not at all. Please can you advise me on the correct pruning procedure?

It sounds like a bit of a hatchet job, but I'm sure it can be easily remedied. You should aim to create an open, cup-shaped plant, so select four or five suitable branches to be your main framework, and remove the rest completely. Cut your chosen branches back by half, to an outward facing bud, to encourage branching. After this, each year, in winter, remove the oldest and most congested of shoots, making way for younger ones. Now is a good time, but if you have problems with birds eating the shoots, wait until after bud burst, so you can see what has survived their onslaught.

What to do this week

Root crops such as beetroot, parsnips, carrots, turnip and celeriac can all be left in the ground and harvested as you need them. Gradually, though, they will deteriorate as cold and wet weather and hungry pests get at them. So you'll need to lift and store them. There is no need to involve the freezer, though, because this is what root crops were made for. Just sort the good ones and stack them in boxes of sand or coir, somewhere cool, and eat the rest. If you can't be bothered, a mulch and a tarp will help preserve them in the ground.

If the ground is not sodden, give your vegetable patch a rough seeing to before the hard frosts. Those who have sandy soil may stay in the warm and abandon all thoughts of digging till spring, but with heavy clay soil you really must force yourself to get out there. Just turn over great big clods, then sit back and let the January and February frosts turn them into fine, crumbly soil ready for spring planting.

This is the time of year when a tree's stake really earns its money. Make sure yours is up to the job. It should be positioned on the windward side of the tree, so that the stem blows away from it, and tree and stake should be tied with a proper tree tie at about one third of the tree's height. Stakes are necessary only on trees planted in the last couple of years, but if you think you've left yours too long, this is not the moment to set it free. Wait until calmer times come in the spring.

Winter

It may seem like there is nothing much going on in the garden in winter, but this is actually the time you can make the most impact on the overall look of your garden. Bare-root trees, shrubs, roses and fruit trees become available as soon as the leaves drop, making this an exciting time for planting. The absence of leaves makes it easy to see where your garden is lacking backbone, and where a bit of structural planting would make a huge difference. Deciduous plants that are already growing in the garden can be moved, if they really need to be, while their leaves are down. They may still struggle to get re-established, but doing it now will give them the best chance.

If your garden looks dull now – and most do so don't be disheartened – consider planting evergreens for structure, as well as shrubs and trees with colourful winter bark, such as cornus, willow and birch. Plant hellebores and winter flowering shrubs for scent, such as hamamelis and daphne. If you don't have any snowdrops in your garden, you should have. They are cheap to buy in bulk and brighten up an otherwise very dull time of year. Just after flowering is the perfect time to plant them, as most are sold while still green to ensure they have the best chance to establish themselves in their new home.

Plants in pots should be lifted up on pot feet, to prevent them getting waterlogged, and grouped together to protect each other from the cold. Lift or wrap any slightly tender plants and keep tender plants in greenhouses on the dry side, as it is often winter wet that does for them.

For vegetables there should be some stored produce such as potatoes and dried beans, but there may be some fresh salad leaves, leeks, carrots, celery, spinach, Oriental vegetables and kale, among others. Anything leafy will produce better quality leaves for longer if grown under a mini cloche. Sow broad beans throughout winter, and plant out garlic in early winter. Garlic can struggle with wet soils over winter, so if you have a clay soil it can be a good idea to plant into modules and keep them in the cold frame or in a sheltered spot. The garlic will sprout and start growing, and can be planted out into its final growing spot come spring.

Winter is a good time to clean up and oil all of your tools, and to check that everything is in good working order. Get your mower serviced now; if you only realise it's broken in spring, you will find yourself at the back of a long queue waiting to get it fixed.

When cold weather strikes, put out food that is high in fats, such as grated cheese and peanuts, to help birds to make it through long, cold nights. Ponds will freeze in very cold weather so float a ball on the surface to try and keep at least a small portion unfrozen, ensuring that any creatures lurking beneath don't struggle for oxygen.

One of the great treats of winter for the gardener is sitting down with a few favourite catalogues and planning the following year's growing. It is worth making a rough sketch of the area you have to fill, and thinking seriously about where each plant is going to go. It is all too easy to order and sow masses of seeds and end up with nowhere to put them. It's nice to have a few plants to give away, but you will save yourself quite a massive amount of work if you keep the numbers down.

Beginning of December

Are there any badger-friendly ways of getting rid of badgers? They have attacked my potato crop, my bluebell bulbs and my newly planted colchicums, as well as nightly digging holes in my lawn.

Sorry to kick you when you're down, but a badly kept lawn contains more grubs, and so is more tempting to the furry garden-trashers. Scratch out dead grass with a spring-tined rake, spike, then brush in sand and topsoil, and apply fertiliser. Installing an electric fence sounds extreme, but they work and are useful around tempting areas, such as a vegetable patch. Badgers forage around the garden most when they need food during cold or dry spells, so you could try feeding them at these times with peanuts, bread or soft fruits. Obviously, however, this could well backfire and just egg them on. Alternatively, try a 1.25m chain-link fence that continues at least 50cm below ground. They are determined critters, however, and this may be a waste of time and money.

I have a young monkey-puzzle tree about 2ft tall, grown from seed by my mother. I am moving house and would like to take it with me because it has sentimental memories. Is this possible?

Monkey-puzzles don't like disturbance, but success rates are higher in younger trees. Wait until the last moment, don tough gloves and protective clothing to avoid getting speared, and dig it up, taking plenty of soil with it. Wrap the root in a piece of tarpaulin and keep it moist. Then get it straight into the ground at the new house, and keep it well watered for the whole of the following year. They are big trees (up to 25m tall), so don't plant under electricity lines or too close to buildings. Their beauty, if that's not too strong a word, is in their final shape, and too many people end up hacking off the tops, making them look awkward and ugly.

Every year my pear tree flowers beautifully, but the tiny fruits that form each have a hole in them. They then go brown and drop off. The man at the garden centre says we should pick the pears and destroy them. We have been doing this for years!

This sounds like pear gall midge. The midges lay eggs in the flower buds, and then the maggots feed on the fruitlets before dropping to the soil, where they overwinter. Your garden centre man is right – you must burn the pears – but don't leave this too late – by mid-summer, the pests may have dropped. You can also try turning over the soil under the tree now and in summer to expose the pests to birds and the elements.

I have several hebes, which are becoming rather tall and sparse. However, I am rather tentative when it comes to pruning. When is the best time to do it? And do they also need deadheading?

Hebes generally need very little pruning, but if they turn leggy, as yours seem to have done, they can be pruned back pretty hard (this is also worth a go if the plants are lacking in flowers). The best time to tackle this job is during that stage of the year after the brunt of winter has passed but before new growth starts in spring. Cut back the plant all over. Big, bushy plants can be cut back to about a foot all over and they should produce new shoots in spring. Deadheading keeps plants looking neat, but is also a good way of helping to keep them bushy, because it stimulates growth from farther down the stems. Do this every year immediately after flowering.

I understand there are some flowers and herbs you can put beside certain plants to keep bugs away. Is there a book that could help me?

You can't go wrong if you plant smelly things, because they'll confuse pests that hunt by scent. Lavender, thyme, French marigold and chamomile are all good bets, so plant them in abundance. There is, of course, much more to it than that, and a good place to discover the intricacies of this fascinating subject is Bob Flowerdew's *Complete Book Of Companion Gardening* (Kyle Cathie). For a wider perspective, any vegetable book with an organic bent will cover companion planting to some extent. HDRA's *Encyclopedia Of Organic Gardening* (Dorling Kindersley), Andi Clevely's *The Allotment Book* (Collins) and Bob Flowerdew's *Organic Bible* (Kyle Cathie) all do so, and also cover other organic pest-control methods, such as the use of physical protection and biological control. All are pretty handy places to start, as is, dare I say it, my own *The Half-Hour Allotment* (Frances Lincoln).

Our ivy is at least 10 years old, but it produces no flowers or berries. I want a wildlife-friendly garden and am wondering if a different ivy would be a better bet.

Your ivy is still in its juvenile climbing, twining and all-conquering phase – it takes at least 10 years for ivy to get large and established enough to enter its mature flowering and fruiting stage. When this happens, the whole form of the plant changes, the leaves lose their lobes and turn lighter in colour, and the plant takes on a bushier appearance. However, this switch is not inevitable. The trigger is thought to be an increase in light (such as that which an ivy climbing up a tree would receive as it neared the top). If your ivy is in dense shade, therefore, it may never actually flower, so cut away any overhanging branches and growth to increase its access to sunlight. Alternatively, you can buy 'tree ivies', which are plants that have been propagated from mature ivies and will flower and fruit from a young age – they are sold as Hedera helix 'Arborescens'. Try Beeches Nursery (beechesnursery.co.uk) or your local garden centre.

What to do this week

Early, pale pink, tender rhubarb stalks can be yours – and all you need to get them is a shed and some decent-sized clumps. Lift and pot up (at least three-year-old) plants now and leave them outside until they have been subject to a couple of hard frosts. Then bring them into the shed or cellar and drape black polythene over chairs, with the plants underneath, to exclude light. After about six weeks, you can begin harvesting the stalks. In spring, when you are finally sick of crumble, plant your rhubarb back into the vegetable garden and don't harvest for the rest of the year.

Living willow rods can make an instant windbreak to stop winter breezes buffeting your patch. Their stems create intricate interest in winter, and are covered in a fuzz of fresh green in summer. Rods are cut and planted, which means pushing them into the ground while the plants are dormant and the leaves are off the stems. Musgrovewillows. co.uk sells kits containing everything you need to make a living tunnel, arbour or dome.

You can do more harm than good at the moment if you are too keen. Two things to bear in mind now: don't dig during or after wet weather, because it will only compact the soil and ruin its structure and don't walk on the lawn when it is frosty, because you will turn the grass to mush and leave muddy footprints.

Early to mid December

We have about 1,000m² of ex-pasture land that we want to clear of brambles, nettles and other perennial weeds. What is the quickest way to do this? We are willing to use weedkiller but would rather not.

You have many hours of backbreaking digging ahead of you. Nettles are relatively easy to dig out: chop them down first, leaving about 1ft of top growth, to prevent yourself from getting stung while you work, then use a fork to dig out the clump, taking as much root as possible. Brambles are more tenacious: established clumps and roots can be hard work to remove, and it is likely that you will have to repeat the operation several times. On a smaller area, you could cover roughly cleared soil with a light-excluding fabric or plastic to kill off remaining weeds, but this should be left in place for at least a year.

I have a large trellis that is empty in winter as the clematis ('William Kennett') lasts only over summer. What colourful thing could I plant for winter to cover the bare lower stems in summer?

There aren't many winter-flowering climbers, so try for some evergreen foliage interest – perhaps a coloured-leaf ivy such as the golden-yellow Hedera 'Buttercup'. You could plant evergreen winter-flowering Clematis cirrhosa, which produces bell-shaped creamy green flowers, or its cultivar 'Freckles' (spotted inside). For summer cover, try cheerful annual climbers such as sweet peas, black-eyed Susan or the Spanish flag, Ipomoea lobata. You may be getting excessively bare stems through a lack of pruning. Large-flowered, early clematis such as 'William Kennett' flower mainly on stems produced the previous year. Many people don't prune them at all, resulting in the flowers being borne higher and higher up. In late winter, cut back to a bud. Reduce a few of the stems quite far down, to encourage new growth from the base, which will bear flowers the following year.

We have a thriving oak tree in our garden. We love it, but it's getting bigger than we'd like. It is around 12m tall, blocks out light and is only 15m or so from the back wall of our house. Is there any way to prune it or prevent further growth?

I spoke to Neville Fay, principal consultant at the Treework Environmental Practice in Bristol (treeworks.co.uk) and chair of the Ancient Tree Forum. Oaks this size can sometimes be reduced by up to 20 per cent, he says, and winter dormancy is the time to get down to work. However, you should be aware that once you start, you will need to keep it up, with maintenance pruning every three to five years. As he says, sagely, 'This is the commitment you need to make to have a forest tree as a garden tree.' A scaled, staged reduction, again with pruning every three to five years, might be better for the tree. A local qualified arborist can assess the possibilities – go to the Arboricultural Association website (trees.org.uk) to find someone in your area.

What is the correct way to overwinter pelargoniums?

One traditional method is to force them to rest by shaking all soil from the roots, leaving them to dry out, then popping them into paper bags and storing in a cool but frost-free, dark place (shed, garage or basement) before re-potting them in spring. The theory is that the fleshy stems keep the plant alive while the temperature suspends growth. However, I have to admit it didn't work for me when I tried it with just a couple of plants, though it would be worth a go if you have lots of plants but little space. If you have just a couple, treat them as houseplants and place them on your coolest, sunniest windowsill. A porch would be ideal, or any room that isn't kept too hot, such as a spare room. Check the soil and leaves carefully for pests first and keep fairly dry over winter, increasing watering in spring.

I've always found sprouts reliable, but last year's crop was an almost total failure, with only a few sprouts the size of a fingernail. I sowed 'United'. Any suggestions?

Brussels sprouts are one of the few cases where it always pays to fork out on expensive F1 hybrid seed, the result of the first cross between two inbred parents. 'United' is an old-fashioned variety, and while the seeds are much cheaper (and can often yield larger sprouts and a better flavour), they are generally much less reliable and more prone to such problems. The sprouts will 'blow' more quickly if not picked as soon as they are ready, and the whole plant is generally not as high quality. There is just time to sow a late variety of a good F1 such as 'Exodus F1' (try fothergills.co.uk) or 'Wellington F1' (organiccatalogue.com).

Why do my limes drop? I bought a small Tahitian lime tree with flowers and fruit. I repotted it, fed it with citrus feed and was careful not to let it dry out, but all the limes fell off and the leaves became lighter in colour. Can I prevent this from happening next time it flowers?

Fruit drop in citrus plants happens most often as a result of a significant change in temperature, most likely from warm to cold, but also the other way around – for instance, when you bring a plant into a heated house at the end of summer after having it outside. As the problem occurred soon after you bought your lime, the chances are the temperature change from nursery to garden centre to home was not as smooth as the plant would have wished. Perhaps it got cold being carried from the heated garden centre to your house. Some unscrupulous nurseries are naughty and grow plants 'soft', which means giving them especially warm temperatures to make them grow quickly and be ready for sale sooner, or fetch a higher price. Growers know that gardeners cannot produce the same conditions at home and that plants will suffer, but they still do it. If you think this is the case, speak to the garden centre. To encourage a new flush of flowers, give the plant as much direct sunlight as possible in spring and summer, even moving it outdoors as soon as you're sure it's warm enough for it not to get a further shock.

What to do this week

A number of trees and woody plants are traditionally pruned before Christmas, among them vines, Japanese maples, birch, walnut and mulberry. This is because pruning them after Christmas, when their sap starts rising (the first sign of spring, anyone?), could potentially weaken them. It's all to do with the amount of sap they 'bleed', and these guys are heavy bleeders, so prune them now while they're still properly dormant. Pruning on trees is likely to be minimal anyway, but if you want to create a clear stem, tidy up any crossing branches or open up canopies of any of these, now is your moment.

Time for a disease-busting clear-up. Leaves dropped by roses are notorious for harbouring diseases such as black spot, and should be raked up and disposed of. Fruit lying beneath trees can also be a source of re-infestation by pests come spring – cut it up and leave out for blackbirds, or compost it. Diseased leaves need to be disposed of with more care: the perfect excuse for a garden fire to warm up a chilly or overcast day.

If you're about to bring in your 'living' Christmas tree, which has been outside in a pot all year, give it at least three pre-sitting room days in a garage or shed. This will help to lessen the shock to its system before it gets to do its annual looking-pretty stint. Indoors, heat sources such as open fires and radiators (even the TV during those Only Fools And Horses marathons) are desiccating, so keep the tree well away from them, and give it plenty of water. You can smooth the passage of its new year eviction by carrying out the same conditioning before putting it out.

Mid December

I have an apple tree that bears no fruit, but has a grand annual crop of mistletoe that has now started to colonise my productive apple trees. Should I be eradicating it?

Mistletoe expert Jonathan Briggs, who runs mistletoe.org.uk, says that mistletoe and apple trees can happily coexist provided the mistletoe is properly managed. Prune back some of the male and female plants each year: if you take only a little from the female, berry bearing plants each Christmas, the males will soon take over, leaving no apples or mistletoe. Rub off new seedlings each summer, before they get established. On the productive trees, just keep cutting it back whenever it appears. You live in Essex, where mistletoe is less rampant than in its West Country stronghold, so give it a little slack.

We planted three rows of 'Autumn Bliss' raspberries on our allotment two years ago. The fruit so far has been disappointing – crumby and partly developed. The other plots have good, large fruits. What could be wrong?

If summer was particularly hot and dry, this would have hit at the same time as the fruit was forming, and this can affect fruit size. The most likely explanation, however, is virus. There are several that affect raspberries, and one of the symptoms is distorted fruit that doesn't fully develop. 'Autumn Bliss' should flower and fruit in its first year, so I would guess they were infected when you bought them (try your supplier for a refund or replacement), although there is a possibility of infection via aphids after planting. I'm afraid they will need to be dug up and new canes planted elsewhere on the plot.

I have an olive tree in a pot on a south-facing patio. I repotted it in September, and it threw out 10 branches. Do I prune it, and how much?

Cut back the sprouts and shape as you like, in spring or summer. Pot on every couple of years in spring, with lots of drainage. Water and feed well when in growth, but allow almost to dry out in winter. Getting fruit is trickier: in spring, select three or four branches as the main framework, shorten by about a third and remove the rest. Hopefully they'll supply flowers and fruit. Each year, allow a few more branches to grow, and remove the oldest after a few years. Olives need winter cold to flower and fruit (at least two months below 10°C) and they also need a long, hot season in order to ripen the fruits.

Three years ago I planted a red-berried pyracantha against a fence to brighten up a dark corner and deter intruders. The plant looks very healthy now, but it has never flowered, so there are no cheery berries. How can I get it to flower?

In deepest shade, pyracantha will grow well enough but will not flower, and so won't produce berries. It doesn't transplant well, either, so you'd probably lose it if you moved it. So leave it where it is, appreciate its burglar-repelling qualities and plant something else for interest. Plants that flower in deep shade include Daphne laureola (not as smelly as its relatives, but pretty), Aucuba japonica (brightly dappled foliage) and trusty old Hydrangea anomala subsp. petiolaris (the climbing hydrangea, white-flowered). Or grow a variegated ivy through the pyracantha.

Do any garden shredders work by hand rather than on electricity? It seems silly to use electricity when I'm trying to be environmentally 'good' by making my own compost.

This is such a good idea, but I've been unable to find one. Woody waste is a problem without a shredder: it won't rot in the compost heap, and it slows down everything else. Another (and even more ecofriendly) approach is to create a 'dead hedge', which makes a feature of such material. Hammer two rows of chestnut stakes into the ground 30cm apart, then lay woody waste, ivy stems, perennial weeds and anything else you can't compost along its length. It provides a home for a bevy of beasties. It will rot down (*very* slowly) but you will be adding to the top all the time, anyway.

We need a low-maintenance answer for a sloping area that's covered in black tarpaulin and bark chippings, which slide down, leaving unattractive bare patches. The ground's too solid to cultivate. Is there such a thing as sticky bark or gravel?

There is resin-bound gravel, but you can't lay it on bare earth and it's very ugly. Sometimes plants are the best low-maintenance option, and I bet you could make a couple of planting holes if you really tried. That tarpaulin set-up will have killed off most weeds, so you have a head start. As this is gardening for someone who hates gardening, I offer you ivy, the resin-bound gravel of the plant world. Deep green Hedera hibernica is almost weed-proof once it's established. If you want something ever so slightly fancier, go for the big, glossy leaves of H. colchica or one of its variegated cultivars.

I am contemplating buying a north-facing piece of land and I want to grow trees and flowers. It is quite a gentle slope (40 degrees) and does get sunlight, but is this enough for growing sun-loving flowers?

As long as it is open enough and not shaded by tall buildings or trees that cast shade, you can grow sun-lovers on a north-sloping piece of land. The problem will be that the soil will take much longer to warm up in spring and will cool down faster in autumn, compared with that on a south-facing slope. This gives you a shorter growing season and leads to later seed germination, bulb emergence and new shoot growth. So, yes, it is possible, but it is certainly not the ideal growing situation.

What to do this week

You didn't force bulbs for your Christmas table display? For shame. Still, there are months of winter blues yet to fend off. Pretty, fragrant paperwhites need no chilling and take just six weeks to bloom.

For a rustic and wildlife-friendly take on outdoor festive decoration, make some bird-food garlands. Ingredients could include slices of apple and orange, whole peanuts, grapes, raisins, chunks of corn on the cob and pine cones spread with peanut butter or suet. Use a large darning needle to thread them on to some string, kebab-style, tying occasional knots as spacers, then drape in trees and bushes.

When you're lopping off bits from holly and other evergreens to add to the indoor decorations, spare a thought for the poor plants, and not just for your boughs and garlands. Don't cut during frosty conditions, and always prune back to a point just beyond a leaf joint, otherwise the leftover stumps may cause disease problems. Don't wreck the plant's shape, either – remember, you'll be looking at it long after the festivities are over – and also make sure you leave a few berries for the birds. Having said that, if your holly has no berries, that means it is either male or lacking a pollinator. Take a sprig to your garden centre to sex it and pair it up.

Late December

Our Photinia 'Red Robin' has black spots on the green leaves, as does some holly. What do you think is causing this?

Photinia leaves often get these purplish black spots after winter, especially after a particularly cold one. As long as the new leaves emerge clean, you have nothing to worry about. I am not quite so confident about your holly, however. If the damage is starting at the bottom of the plant and working its way up, this may be holly leaf blight, which can cause severe defoliation. Prune out some of the denser growth (yes, ouch) to increase airflow, and gather up and burn any fallen leaves. Feed and mulch. Plants usually recover

We have a plum tree that is bearing fruit, but it has been neglected and is in need of pruning. When is the best time to do this?

Although it is heartbreaking when the tree is full of plums, summer is actually the best time to prune. This is because of silver leaf disease, the spores of which are around in greatest number in winter. On most trees, 'wound paints' (such as Growing Success Prune & Seal) are not worth the bother, but there is still a slight disease risk in summer, so apply immediately after cutting. Plum pruning is straightforward and does not require the horticultural acrobatics of, say, apple pruning: just take out weak, damaged or dead branches, as well as any crossing the centre of the tree. Air should flow freely through the branches. On neglected trees, carry this out over several years.

I have propagated a kiwi fruit plant from seed, which now stands at 50cm tall in a 20cm pot. Does it need re-potting and what is its best site?

Kiwis are surprisingly hardy and will survive out of doors over winter in a sheltered spot with lots of sun. You can either put yours into a large pot (they grow very fast) filled with a compost such as John Innes No 3, or plant it straight into the ground, as long as the soil is well drained. Mix in some horticultural grit if you are concerned about drainage. You will need to provide a large sturdy structure for it to grow over. However, if you are hoping for fruit, you are going to be disappointed. This is not because of our climate, but because you need a male and a female plant to get fruit. Having grown yours from seed, you could have either. So how do you sex a kiwi? It is pretty much impossible until the flowers appear, and that will take a few years from seed. Once they do appear, the centres of the male flowers are a mass of stamens, and will produce yellow pollen. The females have these stamen-like structures, too, but they do not produce pollen, and their flowers have a prominent, white, star-shaped structure at their centre. Whichever one you have, you will need to plant the other for pollination and fruiting to occur. If this sounds a bit long-winded, you can always start again and buy a named male cultivar (such as 'Tomuri') and a named female (such as 'Hayward').

We have a large swimming pool in the garden, which was there when we bought the house. The grandchildren are big fans, but we like gardening. Can we grow vegetables and roses in big boxes?

Small, patio-type roses can be grown in containers (see apuldramroses.co.uk), and you can grow lots of veg next spring, including dwarf french beans, carrots, tomatoes, peppers, lettuces, radishes, courgettes and herbs. I am skating over your question because what I really want to talk about is that pool. Why not convert it into a natural swimming pond, thereby turning a chlorinated desert into a beautiful, plant-filled, wildlife-friendly grandchild-pleaser? These are usually built from scratch, but you can convert an existing pool by creating two planting areas with water-filtering plants. The plants do all the work, meaning no more fuss with chemicals, natural water to swim in, plus lots of planting fun. Visit gartenart.co.uk for ideas.

We keep finding toadstools in our Devon garden, and are concerned because we have young children. The garden is on a bank topped by a hedge and two oak trees.

In rural locations, there are loads of fungi teeming in the soil, and many produce nonpoisonous toadstools and are beneficial to the garden. They may be poisonous (for which I can only recommend vigilant removal, then education), but another worry is that they may be a sign that one of the trees is dying, leaving dead roots below the surface. The only way to know for sure is to have the toadstools identified by a local expert; in the meantime, look up spindle shank, shaggy pholiota and sulphur tuft, which are found on decaying wood, and honey fungus, which attacks and kills living wood. If you identify any of these, call in an arboriculturist.

My neighbour says a ladybird-like beetle is destroying all my plants. She says I have to get rid of the plants and start again or squash the beetles (which look just like ladybirds to me).

Your neighbour may be thinking of the harlequin ladybird, first spotted (sorry) in the south-east in 2004 and spreading north and west. It comes in various colour forms and it *doesn't* eat plants; it does eat aphids, though. It has a longer breeding season than native ladybirds, so there is a worry it might out-compete them. That's about it, though – not quite the apocalyptic vision painted by your neighbour. Don't kill them or rip out all your plants.

What to do this week

Christmas Day and Boxing Day are the traditional days for sowing onions. This is far cheaper than growing from sets and allows you to grow lesser-known varieties such as 'Walla Walla', a sweet and mild old French variety that is available only as seed (organiccatalogue. com). Sow on to the surface of fine, moist compost and place in a heated propagator. And if you find you're just a tad busy over the next few days, you can also sow throughout January.

Compost bin overflowing with festive peelings? Start a bean trench. This is the traditional way of keeping hungry, thirsty beans satisfied all summer. Dig a deep trench, then line with layers of newspaper. Water. Tip in some rotted compost and some partially rotted, then chuck in your fresh kitchen scraps throughout winter (but not the rat attractants such as egg shells, meat, fish and cooked stuff, obviously). Come spring, backfill and plant. Don't like runner beans? Do the same on a smaller scale for squashes.

Before you lob your mistletoe into the compost bin, try germinating the seeds. Apple trees are the best hosts, but it is worth a go on others. Choose berries that have turned white (green ones may not be ripe) and are still fleshy, and smear them on to the surface of the bark (crags and fissures can be too gloomy for germination). If successful, it will be two long years before you even see leaves and all of five before any berries put in an appearance, but it'll be worth the wait. Go to mistle.co.uk for more information and for pre-implanted trees.

End of December / beginning of January

Is it OK to put the ash from smokeless coal in the compost bin? Is it OK to put any coal ash in the compost bin?

Neither coal ash nor smokeless fuel ash should be put near soil, says Jim Lambeth of the Solid Fuel Association, as they contain a variety of trace elements and heavy metals that should not be used where foodstuff is grown. Pure wood ash from fires made from untreated and unpainted wood doesn't have these problems, but who has purely wood fires? If you do, it can be put to use, but not on the compost heap. For one thing, there is nothing to rot down, so it is just taking up space, and it would also make the compost more alkaline. It is simpler to sprinkle it where it will be useful. Being high in potash, it will encourage fruit trees and bushes to flower and fruit, and make its presence felt around tomatoes, peas, beans and courgettes.

I have a pyracantha in an old dustbin – good drainage, compost, water occasionally. Why do the berries fall off?

Although in theory anything can be grown in a container, as long as it's big enough, pyracantha is a pretty poor choice. It is large, with an ungainly habit, and I imagine it is a nightmare to keep upright. It will quickly outgrow even your generous dustbin. With only occasional watering, the berry problem is almost certainly down to dryness at the roots. Irregular watering means that the plant has no idea when it is going to get its next drink. With no access to the ground, shedding berries is one of the few things it can do to conserve moisture and save itself. If you can plant it out, please do, and find something more appropriate for your bin. Otherwise, at least give it regular water. A drip hose and timer would keep it happy.

I've had about 120 blooms from my nerines this year. The large bulbs in the centre don't flower, just the smaller ones around the edge. Are the large ones no longer of any use? Friends have asked for bulbs. How do I propagate?

Nerine bulbs love being squashed together in a big crowd, and it is only once they reach this congested state that they'll flower at their best – your bumper crop coinciding with this moment is no surprise. They should be divided only when you notice that you are getting markedly fewer flowers than in the previous year. However, seeing as you want generously to share your bounty, you could dig up a small clump to propagate for your friends. Dividing the inner bulbs will revitalise them and help them to flower once more. They should be planted fairly close together (about 10cm) in their new homes, in sun and well-drained soil, and with their necks sticking out.

We have a cage bird feeder containing seeds, used mainly by tits. Two pigeons harass the tits until they spill the seeds on the ground, and then scoop them up. How can we deter the pigeons but retain the tits?

Pigeons are ground feeders, and though your feeder has been designed to keep pigeons away from the seed, it cannot stop them harassing others. However, these bullies will find somewhere else to feed if they are unsuccessful for a week or two. You could withhold all food, but that seems cruel on the tits. You need to create some sort of barrier that captures the fallen seed, preventing the pigeons from picking it up from the ground. A wire cage (such as those used to take cats to the vet) weighed down with stones, or a pile of large smooth cobbles from the garden centre placed directly under the feeder would deny the pigeons access to their stolen loot. They will eventually get bored and frustrated and go away.

I have an 80-year-old sycamore at the end of my 10m garden. After a dispute with my neighbours, they let five of its seedlings root along our boundary. All are now 4.5m high. I fear the garden will soon be in full shade. Is there any solution?

Little can be done unless the trees start causing trouble, but even then there is no automatic right to light, although if they shade windows you may be able to make a case. You can chop back any limbs or roots that stray into your garden (you must offer them back to your neighbour) and can charge them for work to correct subsidence or drain damage caused. You could warn them of this, but that would really wind them up, particularly as you have your own rather large tree. Why not contact a local mediation service and try to sort out the dispute?

Can you suggest an organic way to deal with weeds on a long path made up of small pavers?

Weeds in lush, moist soil may grow big, but they're easy to pull out. In dry soil, or in cracks, they grow tiny but seem to grip on, making them harder to remove. Repointing the path is the long-term solution. Alternatively, buy a weed knife, which hooks out weed roots. Flame weeders will burn off top growth, but you may end up tackling the same plants again and again. If the path is near the kitchen, pour any leftover boiling water over them each time you make a cup of tea. Reader Kathleen Dickinson suggests salt: she buys a large bag, snips a hole in one corner and puts some on each weed. This has the added advantage of killing slugs.

What to do this week

Forget feasting your eyes – this time of year is all about noses. Flowers need to attract insects, but winter weather batters showy petals, so instead of taking the risk, they pull out of the hat some of the year's best olfactory treats. If your garden is lacking in interest, consider introducing a few star turns, such as Sarcococca confusa, Viburnum x bodnantense 'Dawn', Viburnum farreri, daphnes and mahonia, all of which will get you out there, eyes closed, nostrils flaring.

Now is the time of year when gardeners everywhere have to take a deep breath and get down to the business of pruning their fruit trees (all except peaches, nectarines and plums). Remove crossing and rubbing branches first, then look to the long, whippy growth arising from the main stems. Count three buds along them from the main stem, then cut. It may seem a bind now, but come late summer, these fruiting spurs will do you proud.

If there are any needles left on your Christmas tree, lop off and store the branches before disposing of the rest in an eco-friendly manner (the correct answer is community shredding and composting, by the way). They are perfect for draping over foolish bulbs and perennials that get carried away by mild spells and think spring has come early. This leaves those eager little shoots exposed to the ravages of chilly weather later on, and a coniferous blanket provides both insulation and good airflow.

Early January

Over the past few years, my red and white currants have suffered from blister aphid attacks. Do you have any suggestions for an organic pesticide?

Currant blister aphid damage is characterised by a distinctive puckering of the leaves. Blister aphids overwinter on the bark of trees, so are good candidates for a winter tree wash. The gruesome tar oil washes that used to be employed are no longer available, but they have been replaced by an organic alternative: Growing Success Winter Tree Wash (try greengardener.co.uk) is based on plant oils and dissolves eggs with which it comes into contact. It must be applied while the tree is dormant or new growth will be harmed, so carry out one wash now and another in February. It doesn't have the persistence of the old washes, however, so application must be thorough. Do it on a calm day to prevent damage to nearby plants.

In my polytunnel last year my strong, healthy tomato and french bean plants did not produce a harvest at all – the few tomatoes I did get were tiny. I also noticed a great lack of insects, even though I garden with wildlife in mind.

Tomatoes and beans need pollinators, and plants in polytunnels exclude insects – even with the doors open, you will have fewer than outside. The general lack of insects is worrying, but installing an insect house now (near the doors) will help them, and you. The experts are mason bees and bumble bees – greengardener.co.uk supplies homes. Entice them into the garden with nectar-rich plants such as geraniums, borage, deadnettles and feverfew, and make life easy by providing a pile of moistened, sifted mud as nest-building material. If it takes a while for numbers to build up, help the tomatoes pollinate by buzzing an electric toothbrush against the flower stems for a second or two.

I am thinning overgrown rhododendrons, clearing the ground and leaving a canopy for a woodland area. Is it true that nothing will grow where rhododendrons have been?

Rhododendron roots and leaves contain growth inhibitors that stop other plants from thriving, so where they have grown over a long period, the build-up of debris can make life hard going for new plants. Remove the top layer of soil, and ameliorate what's left with garden compost or mushroom compost. One theory is that rhododendrons inhibit the mycorrhizal fungi that work in tandem with roots, so a boost with Root Grow won't hurt. Foxgloves seem to be immune to rhodo poisoning, so plant them in the meantime

I laid a lawn when my house was new, on clay soil built up from waste from the housing development, and have faced a constant battle against perennial weeds and bad drainage. I want to lay a new lawn in spring. How can I keep it weed-free?

The vigorous growth of lawn grasses combined with regular mowing usually keeps lawn weeds under control. But the success of any lawn is in its preparation, and yours had a particularly inauspicious start. Your soil is made up of dumped clay subsoil that the builders wanted shot of, which is dreadful stuff on which to plant anything. Its poor drainage will have slowed growth in the lawn, allowing the weeds to get a hold. Remove any perennial weed roots, then spread several tonnes of topsoil over your soil, ideally a few inches deep, before treading it down and returfing. To maintain good drainage, spike your lawn all over every autumn with a fork, and brush in a mixture of topsoil and sand.

I want to grow a fruit tree, espalier-style, along a sunny wall. I have room for only one, though, so would appreciate some advice as to what to go for.

I would be tempted to choose one of the new apricot cultivars – they have been bred for UK conditions and produce much sweeter, juicier fruit than you normally find in the shops. They are a real treat. Choose from 'Tomcot' and 'Delicot'. Bear in mind that those trees really need a light, free-draining soil to do well, so on a heavier soil consider a cherry. 'Stella' and 'Sunburst' are self-fertile and produce tonnes of pretty blossom in spring and sweet, deepest red fruit in late summer that will look wonderful dripping from the horizontally trained branches of an espalier. Both are fairly compact when trained this way, but if you're short on space, look for fruits grown on the new Gisela 5 rootstock, which will stay much smaller than those on traditional Colt. Try keepers-nursery.co.uk.

I am using an old, 60cm-long tin bath as a pond. It contains a ramp (so animals can climb out on to a nearby raised bed), a grass and a buttercup. Disappointingly, after a year, I've still not attracted any frogs or toads, and the water contains a green, mossy slime.

Oxygenating plants will help rid you of the slime – ask at your local garden centre. As for your pond's lack of frogs and toads, sometimes they just take a couple of years to find new ponds. However, frogs hibernate underwater and need a deep pond that won't freeze solid. You may have more luck with toads, which winter on land. They want shade from the sun in hot weather, and access to moisture, so plant up your raised bed with sheltering vegetation, and make a toad hole from an upside-down terracotta pot into which you have drilled out an entrance hole (W: 8cm x H: 4cm), then sink this into the ground in a shady spot. I do, however, wonder how the toads are meant to struggle up on to the raised bed in the first place, but hopefully you've thought of that.

What to do this week

Liming the soil may seem like one of those mysterious activities only for the horny-handed sons of toil at the allotment. But it's a shame more people don't follow the old boys' lead. Lime is magic dust, giving you larger vegetables for almost no effort. The reason? It makes soil more alkaline, allowing plants to unlock hidden nutrients from the earth. Brassicas, peas and beans love it, so sprinkle liberally where these are to grow. Potatoes do not, so don't.

Naturally you have left the stems of your herbaceous plants standing, but they are probably looking a bit ragged by now. There is life (or rather death) in them yet, but they could do with a bit of titivating. Go through each plant selectively with secateurs, taking out only the bent, battered or messy bits, to bring out the best of what's left. As you do it, imagine how beautiful they would look covered in a sparkling rime of hoar frost, and think how gutted you would be if we got one and you had just chopped them all down.

Your grass-clogged lawnmower half-filled with gunky old petrol is going to be in bad shape come spring. Drain the petrol (it will work in the car), clean the innards with a stiff brush and sharpen the blades – this is simplest with a drill attachment (try harrodhorticultural.com). Change the oil, then start the engine. If it doesn't start, take it to the mower repair shop now – if you wait until the grass starts growing, you're likely to find yourself at the end of a very long queue.

Mid January

I need to establish my boundary with next door but don't want panel fencing, and privet puts me in a cold sweat. I would like to encourage wildlife. Have you any suggestions (part of the boundary is in shade)?

A native mixed hedge is great for wildlife, but most British hedgerow plants lose their leaves in winter – no good if you want privacy. Three native plants fit the bill, though. Holly is evergreen and makes a beautiful hedge, full of berries for the birds. Hornbeam and beech are deciduous, but when grown as a hedge, the leaves turn autumnal colours and stay on the plant. Both provide seeds for birds and small mammals. While privet looks the same year round, these two spend spring bright green, summer darker green and winter burnt orange (beech) and brown (hornbeam). All do well in partial shade – find them in tree nurseries and some garden centres. Mix along the length of the hedge for a patchwork of colours and textures. Late winter to early spring is the time to plant. Prune in late winter for three years, then only every few years, to allow fruits and berries to develop. Once established, introduce climbers such as the native honeysuckle (Lonicera periclymenum), which will attract bees and smell wonderful.

We've got a dozen or more molehills in our garden. What can we do?

Mole control comprises two basic approaches: you either trap them and take them elsewhere or annoy them so much that they move away of their own accord. Humane traps are available from garden centres. Use gloves when setting them into the tunnels, as moles will avoid your smell. You must check traps every day, or you can't really call them humane. Sound and smell can both be used as deterrents. There are devices that emit a high-pitched noise, which attracts the curious critters at first, but soon gets on their nerves, making them scarper. Cheaper devices include semi-buried bottles, which make a noise when the wind blows over the open necks, and plastic windmills on sticks. Place them next to or in each molehill. Whiffy deterrents such as garlic, chilli powder, mothballs and castor oil may work faster.

I grow dahlias in pots and bring them indoors each winter. I'd like to take cuttings but don't know how.

Cuttings are a good idea. Dahlias grown from them can produce more and better flowers than those grown from tubers. You need to start your existing tubers growing now by placing in a warm, bright spot in the house and watering. Once the shoots are a few inches high, cut them off down to the base, just below a node (the point on the stem from where the leaves rise). Using a sharp knife or secateurs, remove leaves from the bottom half of the cutting, then push it into a small pot of well-drained compost (mix in vermiculite for extra drainage). Those grown in a heated propagator will root fastest, but in an unheated one they should still root in about four weeks. Move to somewhere cool and frost-free, such as a cold frame or sunny porch, until all danger of frost has passed, then plant out.

My mother has a medium-sized garden that attracts wild birds. Over the past year, five pet cats moved into the neighbourhood and Mum's feathered visitors are being picked off one by one. She is very upset. Can you recommend anything prickly that would make a dense but attractive barrier?

Berberis darwinii has orange flowers, dark-green leaves and is very prickly, while Rosa sericea subsp. omeiensis f. pteracantha has dramatic huge red thorns. It may be a while before either is dense enough for the job, but they would be useful positioned beneath bird-feeding stations so the cats cannot lurk beneath. Birds also need such dense vegetation to escape into when danger threatens.

Make sure your mum isn't putting seed on the ground, and that cats cannot jump on to feeding platforms from other surfaces. Contact the owners and ask them to give their cats collars with bells, and to keep the cats indoors at dawn and dusk, which is when birds are most active. You could also try an ultrasonic device called CATWatch, which has been endorsed by the RSPB and is available in garden centres. It reduces the number of visiting cats by about one third, increasing over time.

I want to grow food in my garden but am worried about the horrors visited upon it over its 115-year history – rampant pesticide use, dumped household chemicals and coal ash, to name but a few. I've gardened it organically for nine years. Does soil clean itself, or should I test it?

They say it's not paranoia if they really are out to get you, and I suppose horrendous chemicals have been passed off as safe over the decades. But bear in mind that even organic farm certification usually only requires a two-year chemical-free period. You are imposing much higher standards on yourself than they do. Rainwater will leach the nasties out of the soil, given time. If your hypothetical Victorian vandals and their successors were into dumping coal ash in the garden, then the soil could be quite acid, making it no use for growing vegetables. You can test this with a home kit, and easily correct it with applications of lime. Unfortunately, today's air pollution, particularly in cities, far outstrips any legacy from our gardening ancestors. Start your vegetable patch, but wash your veggies before eating.

My lemon tree has got colder than it would have liked. It now looks grey and shrivelled and the fruit has turned to mush. Is there anything I can do to restore it or have I killed it?

Lemons are sensitive to frost and it sounds like yours might well be done for. They really need to be moved indoors to a greenhouse or cool conservatory if they are to survive the winter. If you have such a place it is worth trying to save it. Move it there now, and perhaps wrap it up in some horticultural fleece to keep it extra cosy. Reassess in spring, but brace yourself for the worst.

What to do this week

Winter gardening need not be all about future glories. This is the time to plant a tree for winter interest, and you would be hard pressed to beat the Tibetan cherry, Prunus serrula. It has shiny, copper-red bark that peels away as it ages, revealing layers of ever-shinier bark beneath. In spring it has small white blossom. Grow in sun in any soil.

Arm yourself with a heavy stack of seed catalogues, for now is the time to get ordering. Some good ones to help get you started: The Real Seed Catalogue (unusual and hardy vegetable varieties: realseeds. co.uk) Chiltern Seeds (everything you can think of, both ornamental and edible chilternseeds.co.uk) and Seeds Of Italy (gourmet Italian vegetables: seedsofitaly.com).

Mulching your borders thickly now will help to keep the ground cold or frozen. That may sound like madness when you are longing for warmer days, but it helps to guard against the siren call of the premature warm spell. Such a spell tempts soft, delicate buds to start growing, then heartlessly abandons them to later cold snaps. Mulch has more immediate charms, too: it evens out messy borders and is the closest you will get to an instant makeover with that £10 garden voucher.

Late January

I saw an item on TV about small-scale veg growing at the RHS garden in Harrogate. It looked interesting, with mini raised beds. How can I make my small garden productive?

Growing in raised beds, as the RHS does at Harlow Carr, allows you to create a richly fertile soil and so cram crop after crop into a little space. Build your own or buy Link-a-Bords (from harrodhorticultural. com). The tricky part is anticipating spaces as crops finish – no ground should be left fallow if you want to get a decent return. This requires good forward planning. You will find seasonal plans of the Harlow Carr beds in the Grow Your Own section on the RHS website (rhs.org.uk/vegetables). There are numerous books on the subject, but the classic of the genre is *Square Foot Gardening*, by Mel Bartholomew, who started the trend 30 years ago.

My camellia is in a tub in a protected spot, and facing south. It flowered well last year, but the flowers fell off quickly. Is there anything I can do this year to stop this happening?

Camellias are pretty luxuriant flowers to be out so early in the year. Their petals are large and thick, and so are susceptible to damage. Most early bloomers – witch hazels and sarcococcas, for example – are mean in comparison; their thin, insignificant petals are designed to withstand frosts and the beatings of the winter weather. Camellia flowers can cope with the frosts, but what they can't take is the quick thaw when a frost is followed by early morning sunshine. The petals turn to mush, go brown and drop off. In your south-facing spot, it is quite likely that this is the problem. Your camellia is in a pot, so it should be easy to move it somewhere it will get sunshine only from midday onwards. But it would even be worth considering digging up and moving a plant if the problem was really bad. Choose a position against a west-facing wall, to give the petals time to thaw gradually before the sun falls on them.

Is it a bad idea to reuse compost from potted plants, either for repotting or for adding to borders? Also, could I sterilise it by spreading it on a sheet of plastic on a hot day? It seems wasteful to throw it away.

It is a bad idea to repot using old compost, because the nutrients in it will have been used up and its structure will be deteriorating, making it harder to wet. If you are a keen recycler, you could mix in a slow-release fertiliser and fresh garden compost and use it again for one season, but growth may not be as good as with fresh. As for laying the compost out in the sun, some pests that build up in pots might be affected – slug eggs would not last long, and ants' nests would be forced to relocate – so try this if you are thinking of using it again for pots. A much better use for old compost is to dig it into borders, where nutrients are not so necessary and pests are prey to other predators.

I have a fig tree in a large tub. Twice a year it produces large, plump fruit that never ripens. How can I encourage it to fruit successfully?

I know there are some jammy gardeners out there (mainly in London and the south-east) whose trees ripen two crops a year, Mediterranean-style. However, the rest of us have to make do with just the one. Now that the leaves have fallen, have a close look and you will see the two crops in development. There will be some medium-sized fruit and some much smaller, pea-sized ones. The larger fruit are vulnerable to the cold and unlikely to make it through winter undamaged. The pea-sized ones are your future crop. You might think you could hedge your bets and keep both, but it doesn't seem to work like that. You have ruthlessly (and counterintuitively) to remove every larger one now, to make the tree focus on ripening up the little ones next summer.

I am worried about my water butt freezing or overflowing. Should I disconnect it for the rest of winter? I could pipe excess water over evergreens but also have some willows. Would they absorb any water in winter?

Using a proper rainwater diverter (rather than just aiming the drainpipe at the butt) should resolve problems with overflow, because water is automatically diverted down the drain when the butt is full. I have also seen a fantastic set-up involving multiple butts and moveable downpipes, but this still leaves a problem with freezing. It seems a shame to lose all that winter water, but draining is the safest option because freezing can misshape the butt, and they aren't cheap. Do use it on evergreens, which may relish a little extra winter watering. Willows don't absorb water at the rate they do in summer, but they are built for soggy ground so won't mind a bit.

I had a Russian vine over my garage. It flourished for two years, then died. Why?

Its other name is mile-a-minute because it's so ridiculously vigorous. I've never heard of one simply dying. Sometimes recommended without warning by naughty garden centre sales people, it usually takes sustained chemical and physical attacks to kill it: perhaps a neighbour saw it coming and made a pre-emptive strike? Maybe, if it was planted two years ago, its roots were not established, leaving it vulnerable to drought or an animal digging beneath it. Either way, see this as a blessing. It had covered your garage in two years and would not have stopped there. A good alternative is the beautiful, vigorous (but more manageable) Clematis montana and cultivars.

What to do this week

Source potatoes now for chitting in February, and start saving your egg boxes, too. The next couple of weeks will see potato days being held in nurseries and garden centres, where you can get advice and even try samples (a posh way of saying that they might be serving chips). The events give you access to the widest range of the most freshly harvested seed potatoes and are worth a visit even if you have space for only a couple of rows.

Now, you should all have pruned your wisterias once already, in the summer. That first prune would have reduced foliage and allowed the stems to bake and ripen in the sun. The second, winter one further reduces the pruned side growths to a few inches. In the event that you were too busy sunbathing and forgot the summer prune, you can still do the winter one, but in this case keep your stems a little longer, at about six inches.

A thorough greenhouse clean will evict any over-wintering pests and moulds, and also allow the glass to let in the maximum amount of light in advance of spring seed sowing. Choose a mild, sunny day and move any plants indoors temporarily. Start off with the vacuum cleaner on a long extension lead to get into all the corners and crevices, then clean with a scrubbing brush, Jeyes fluid and hot water, before polishing up your panes with a good glass cleaner.

End of January / beginning of February

I've been making compost for over a year and have amassed quite a heap. What do I do with it now?

Don't hang on to it any longer. It needs to be used up to make way for the huge influx of green stuff that will be coming its way with the next growing season. Spreading it over borders sets off winter plants beautifully, helps to improve the soil for spring, but most importantly exposes any beasties (such as slug eggs and snails) for ravenous birds to pick off. Scrub clean every crack and crevice of the bin, and it will be ready to leap into composting action come spring.

I'd like to make a child-safe circular pond and have space for up to only 2m (6ft) square. Is this too small? I would also like to find a metal grill that will support a person's weight. Is this possible?

The larger a pond is, the easier it is to maintain, simply because a larger body of water takes longer to heat up and cool down. However, your pond sounds adequate, so long as you make it between 45cm and 60cm deep to prevent it from freezing solid in winter. Rubber liners are generally better than PVC ones, and either is better than a pre-formed liner, because it is tricky to dig the correct shaped hole for these. A cover is a great idea to make it safe. DiamonDeck (pondsafety.com) will cut their safety grid to the exact shape of your pond. It can be fitted to lie just below the water surface, so from afar it is almost invisible.

I have a couple of things I want to move: a five-foot fatsia that is encroaching on a path, and a clump of cornus bushes that have been cut down annually. Is this possible, and what is the best way?

The cornus bushes, being deciduous, should be moved now, while they're still dormant. Having been cut down regularly, they will not be too large, so will not require pruning. The fatsia, being evergreen, should be left until early spring when new growth is just beginning to emerge. Fatsias respond well to pruning, and yours will cope best with the move if you give it a chop, at least halving its size. Other than timing, the drill is the same: dig the new hole first, take as much root as possible with you, transplant quickly, and water well throughout the following year.

My acacia has grown up to the conservatory roof. Recently, many of its leaves died. I'm not sure about winter watering and feeding. And what is the best size of pot?

A small pot and excessive winter watering might be the cause. I know that's vague, but containers for trees should be as large as possible – free-range tree roots spread beyond the edge of the canopy. You cannot emulate this in a container, but the more it can stretch out, the happier it will be. Aim for a pot at least a couple of feet across and deep – larger, if possible. Consider a raised bed, or an old-fashioned galvanised dustbin with some holes in the base. Winter watering should be fairly sparse, allowing the compost to dry out in-between. In spring, increase watering and give an occasional feed. You'll need to prune, too, in spring after flowering, and repeat a little every year – they don't like hard pruning.

Our pampas grass is a disappointment. The flowers get waterlogged and the stalks cannot support their weight. We can't burn it because of the proximity to trees and shrubs, but we did try cutting it down three years ago. Everybody else's in the neighbourhood stands up whatever the weather.

How terribly retro. Pampas grass is the horticultural equivalent of the prawn cocktail, and I love the idea that there still exist suburbs where neighbours are surreptitiously comparing clumps. I am being slightly mean, as they have had a bit of a revival of late, planted among other grasses and perennials in naturalistic, prairie-style schemes. The trouble is they are not really suited to this, as they hate being crowded in and shaded out by other plants. What they really want is space, light and a freely draining soil, and so, unfortunately, they thrive when planted as one of those weird lawn islands so beloved of 1970s front gardens. Perhaps this is why your neighbours' pampas looks good while yours is suffering. You might move it to somewhere less shaded (don't even think about that lawn), or move any nearby plants. Finally, you should really be cutting it back every year – they can be burned where there is space around them, but have a bucket of water or hose handy, as they really flare up.

Can you recommend plants for my first-floor balcony? I live by the sea in south Wales. The balcony gets plenty of sun and, in winter, lots of wind.

Your main problem will be damage from salt spray carried by those winds. Salt-tolerant evergreen shrubs that provide interest all year include box and the lovely Pittosporum 'Tom Thumb', with its deep purple and lime-green foliage. Being near the sea and away from the ground, frosts are unlikely to trouble you excessively, so I would be tempted to try a couple of things that are not totally hardy. Yuccas and cordylines tolerate salt and are striking in pots. For flowers, look to plants that grow near the sea in their natural habitats, such as rosemary, rock rose (cistus), broom (cytisus) and sea thrift (Armeria maritima).

What to do this week

Hopefully you had the foresight (or laziness) not to cut back the leaves on your ornamental grasses last autumn, and so have been enjoying their swaying movement all winter. But enough is enough. Deciduous grasses in particular are looking tatty and need a trim, giving the new shoots space to develop without getting tangled in old growth. Cut them close to the ground, taking care not to damage emerging shoots. A feed and mulch will set them up nicely.

Peas and sweet peas can make for a frustrating start to the seed-sowing year. Even placed high on greenhouse shelves or slippery staging in apparently rodent-free gardens, this prized bounty is sniffed out by hungry mice, leaving a row of empty holes. That said, mice are surprisingly fussy – once seeds have germinated, they'll turn their noses up at them – so start seeds off indoors on wet kitchen roll, primary school-style, and pop them into compost as soon as they sprout.

If your summer-flowering clematis have got into a messy tangle, prune them back hard now, to just above a bud, and they will put on lots of new growth in time for a great display of flowers. However, slugs love young, emerging clematis foliage, so be wary of pruning down to the ground and protect the shortened stems with a copper ring (from slugrings.co.uk) – by far the most effective slug barrier and mighty pretty, too.

Early February

I'm about to choose potatoes to chit from last year's crop. Do I get a better crop from large seed, or doesn't size matter too much?

The perfect size is about that of a hen's egg. But you're out on a limb: potatoes are martyrs to diseases, which over time lower yields. So buy seed potatoes from certified virus-free sources. If you still want to try, plant into soil that has been free of potatoes, tomatoes or aubergines for a few years, and has not been recently manured, and keep up a four-year rotation. Plant a few tubers especially for seed potatoes and watch for disease. Cut the foliage in the last week of July (early potatoes) or the middle of August (main crop potatoes), to decrease exposure to viruses and keep them at the requisite egg size. Allow the crop to dry, ideally in the sun, for a few weeks. Buy new tubers when you notice yields decreasing.

My town garden consists of a series of pots, with no possibility of rainwater collection. My tumble dryer collects waste water in a reservoir. Is it safe to use on plants such as camellias and seedlings?

If it's green points you're after, you might be better off ditching the tumble dryer, but it is admirable that you're keen to recycle water. There is no reason why tumble dryer run-off shouldn't be used on most plants – grey water from the washing machine is safe and yours will contain less detergent because it is produced after the rinse cycle. Sadly, it can't be used on the plants you mention. Detergents make water alkaline, and camellias thrive in acidic soil. Seedlings are sensitive to chemicals and detergents. Have you thought of squeezing in a wall-mounted water butt (gardentrading. co.uk or greengardener.co.uk)?

A large clump of Japanese anemones is taking over the garden. I've tried to split the clump and move them, but they wilt and become feeble.

Japanese anemones can be troublesome to move. They need tons of moisture to prevent wilting, and the roots struggle to take up enough water while they re-establish. That said, now is a good time to dig up anemones and take 12cm long root cuttings. Lay on a tray of sandy compost and cover to a depth of 2.5cm. When they start growing, pot individually and plant out after a year.

I have three rose plants that have grown to 2m high. Would it be safe to cut them down to half that size, even though there appear to be no shoots on the lower stems? And when can I do this?

Bush roses tolerate – relish, even – pretty extreme pruning, and now is the time to do it. Although there are currently no shoots lower down, there will be buds. These might stay dormant for ever if you let the plant grow unpruned, but as soon as you cut it back, they will leap into action. To prune, start at the centre of the plant and cut out any crossing stems. Remove any weak growth before cutting back the main stems. Large-flowered hybrid tea roses can be cut back to leave about four buds, but floribundas should be left larger, at about eight to ten buds. Where possible, cut to an outward-facing bud, so the stems grow outwards, thereby creating an open shape. And be bold: roses flower on new growth, so any mistakes are quickly covered.

I am moving to Spain next month and was wondering if there are any plants worth taking from my garden. I have taken cuttings of hydrangeas and have some lovely begonias in pots. Will either of those be happy over there?

It would be worth taking anything you are particularly fond of and giving it a go. Hydrangeas certainly grow well in Spain, and you may find that begonias can live out of doors all year round (in the shade, of course), turning into monster plants. The plants that will struggle most are those that need a really good, long period of cold, so perhaps leave the rhubarb behind. Movement of plants for personal use between EU countries is pretty free, but make sure they are healthy, and free of pests and diseases. However, you are not permitted to take rhododendrons, azaleas, viburnums and camellias, because those plants are hosts of sudden oak death, which is present in Britain but not Spain.

Early every spring, I plant tomato seeds in a heated propagator in my greenhouse. Every year, they grow very tall and thin, with the first flower trusses about 2ft up the stalk. How can I grow short, sturdy plants?

This is a timely reminder for all those kitchen gardeners with greenhouses (or well-lit windowsills and sunny, sheltered gardens) to sow tomato, pepper and aubergine seeds in the next few weeks. Light is the key to producing stocky, well-branched plants. The less light available to them, the more they will stretch upwards to get their fill. Light shouldn't be a problem in a greenhouse, unless it's shaded, in which case move the propagator to a brighter spot or remove whatever is causing the shade (you are wasting the potential of the greenhouse otherwise). You might initially sow the seeds fairly close together in a seed tray, but prick them out into individual pots once they are large enough to handle. Then give each pot plenty of space, as the plants grow fast and can quickly cast shade over their siblings. Here's a tip used by some commercial growers: gently brush the tops of the seedlings once a day with your fingertips – this simulates the wind they would get out of doors, and encourages sturdy growth in response. If your plants still get gangly, plant them deep, removing the bottom leaves and planting up to the next set. The stems will send out roots to stabilise the plant.

What to do this week

This is a good time for planting perennial vegetable plants, including horseradish. Growing this pungent friend of beef couldn't be easier. In garden, as in sandwich, a little goes a long way, and this thug will quickly outgrow its welcome unless restrained in a pot, sunken or otherwise. Look out for the (no less invasive) variegated type with its bizarre and impressive splashed white foliage. If possible, simply beg a small segment from an allotment neighbour with an excess. They will be glad to see the back of it.

Hellebore leaves are doing little work to feed the plant now, just hanging about looking manky. Lopping them off to expose the beautiful flowers is not unduly fastidious. It may actually help the plant by removing hellebore leaf spot spores before they have a chance to infect the new foliage that is just coming through. Don't panic about flopping flowers during cold weather – they are surprisingly tough and will pop back up again as soon as the weather thaws.

Now is the time to start thinking about sowing flower and vegetable seeds. Shuttle trays make it easy to move your seedlings about – useful if you don't have a greenhouse and spend late spring shifting your seedlings in and out of the house. Used by professional growers, each tray consists of 18 x 9cm pots, handy for larger seedlings such as sunflowers, or for pricking out. The pots nestle neatly in the trays, making them easy to fill with compost and preventing them from falling over. They are made from recycled plastic, and each pack contains five trays, giving you 90 pots.

Mid February

Do you have any ideas of what to plant in an old brown ceramic sink?

I would plant the beautiful alpine, or border, auriculas. These are primulas with striking markings, often shaded light to dark in purples, blues, pinks, yellows and even browns. They look lovely planted with ferns. They are small and so are best raised up in a container where you can see them, but often suffer terribly in pots as evil vine weevils love their fleshy roots. They seem to do well in troughs or sinks though, perhaps because the weevil does less direct damage to individuals. Provide light shade at midday and keep the soil moist. Visit auriculas.co.uk for mail order plants.

Birds tear off the moss on my roof tiles, thereby clogging the gutters and littering the conservatory roof. Any effective remedies?

Roof moss has become more prolific in recent years as air quality has improved, and roofs now provide a haven for mosses. Moss harbours insects that provide food for birds, it absorbs rainwater and it slows run-off. A compromise would be to put filters over the tops of the downpipes – you'll still have to clean the gutters, but the pipes won't get blocked with clumps of moss. A traditional remedy is to run copper wire along the ridge of the roof. Rainwater causes copper to oxidise, creating copper sulphate, which runs down the roof and kills moss spores. Copper Ridge (copperridge.co.uk) can help you to this end, if you must.

I recently got an allotment – how do I get rid of an area of thick grass growing through carpet?

Many allotment societies ban carpet – it degrades, leaving bits of underlay and fibre in the soil, and it lets in weeds anyway. The grass on your plot is in all probability couch grass, so the answer is elbow grease, a year or two under black plastic, or chemicals. To dig it out, use a fork – a spade would just chop through the roots. Aim to get out each and every one. Once the soil is fairly clear, plant potatoes. You will then get a chance to pick out any escapees when you earth the potatoes up and, later, harvest them. Couch grass roots can be rotted in water to make potent but pongy fertiliser.

My interlocking block drive is unevenly sinking. As worms excavate beneath and raise sand and soil to the surface, the generous rainfall of west Scotland washes it down the slope. What treatments will stop this activity?

You are on dodgy ground here, if you'll pardon the pun. Worms are the holy cows of the garden: they can do no wrong, or at least nothing to warrant wholesale slaughter. Back in the day, you could have found worm-killer in garden centres (positioned between the spring traps and the sparrow poison, probably), but such products have since been withdrawn from sale. I can't help thinking that the worms are taking a pretty heavy rap, anyway. Can they really undermine a well-laid path? You need to re-lay it, properly. Hire a vibrating plate to compress your underlayer of sand, and once the pavers are in place, vibrate everything again. The pavers should be so tightly packed by now that worms don't stand a chance. Just to make sure, you can brush in some kiln-dried sand and that will seal the job.

I planted a Virginia creeper four years ago to cover a wall made from pre-stressed concrete blocks. The plant is growing well, but will not climb the wall. I have tried pinning it on, but it falls off. Any suggestions?

Really smooth walls can fox Virginia creepers. They cling by self-adhesive pads, but these attach better the rougher the surface. Mix a fine grade of sand into normal masonry paint, or just buy a textured paint – these now come in pretty colours and not just battleship grey. This should provide enough purchase to turn your spreader into a climber. Your plan of pinning the stems to the wall is a good one, because the wind can whip away enterprising stems just as they are getting a toehold. A set of wires, attached to the wall at regular intervals, will allow you to tie them firmly in place.

My roses flowered less well last year than I would have liked. What can I do to rejuvenate them?

Summer is too late to start coaxing reluctant roses into flowering. The time to act is now. If they've been less than spectacular in recent years, they may need a feed. Apply sulphate of potash to toughen up growth and promote flower buds, and give them a dose of bananas. Yes, really – place one or two at the base of each rose, and cover with mulch: the bananas will then rot down and release an enormous dose of flower-promoting potassium. Repeat the exercise when the roses are in full bloom. Where squirrels are a problem, simply bury the fruit deeper or make monthly banana skin smoothies (chopped banana skin and water in a blender), to pour straight on to the roots throughout summer. If this is too odd for you then buy a specially formulated rose fertiliser for application in April and midsummer. Now is also the best time to prune back growth by two-thirds, and remove crossing stems.

What to do this week

One of the year's most satisfying jobs is feeding and mulching, and the moment is upon us. Scatter pelleted chicken manure under all plants, but pay most attention to trees and shrubs and anything that hasn't been flowering too well. Then fork compost or well-rotted manure over the top. The pellets provide the quick hit, sending plants hurtling towards spring in rude health. The manure is for long-term benefit, but its dark, rich covering makes the neglected winter garden look instantly cared for.

In theory, you can start sowing tomatoes, chillies, peppers and aubergines now, but it doesn't pay to be too hasty if you want to plant them outside for the summer: windowsill-grown plants can get leggy if they're left hanging around for the last frost, so it's best to wait until early April. That said, there's no harm in checking out the mouth-watering range on offer at Simpson's Seeds (simpsonsseeds.co.uk).

The perennial weed roots that arise from winter digging are difficult to dispose of, being too wet for a fire and too wickedly persistent for the compost heap. Instead, put them into a bucket with a lid, fill with water and leave for six weeks. The resulting evil-smelling brew makes a good plant feed, and the mush of thoroughly dead roots can be safely chucked on the compost heap.

Mid to late February

I have some apple trees approaching 100 years old, which are attractive and fruit well. However, the branches have started developing a moss-like growth and I wonder if I ought to do something about this. The garden is shaded for part of the day by next door's large chestnut.

Apple trees are thought to be past their best by about 50, after which fruiting starts to decline. But old trees such as yours take on a beauty of their own and would be worth keeping even if they weren't producing good fruit. The moss is almost certainly a result of their age and the shade, and is not a major problem. It might harbour overwintering pests, but equally might provide a home for beneficial insects. Its presence perhaps suggests there is insufficient airflow through the tree – this is easily remedied by pruning. Remove dead or diseased branches, as well as those that cross the centre of the tree, and try to create an open, cup-like shape. The next month or so is a good time to do this. If the growth is particularly dense over summer, prune away some of the outer branches.

Are there any non-toxic ways of destroying the brambles growing among my shrubs?

Digging up the whole lot, shrubs and all, is the only really effective method. You can then work over the border removing every last bit of root before replanting the shrubs. If this is impossible, try repeatedly cutting back the brambles: once in spring, again in summer (when they have put lots of energy into flower production) and a last cut in autumn. However, they are very vigorous and persistent, and you'd need to keep this up for a good few years.

Is there any way of getting rid of Spanish bluebells? They are pleasant enough for a week or two, but it is tedious getting rid of the stems and leaves once they have died.

In the garden, their land-grabbing tendencies are contained, but it is true that they are thuggishly persistent, even resisting the hammer blow of weedkiller. The trick is to deny them their two weeks of glory. By digging them up when they are in leaf, you will find more of the bulbs and underground stems. It will take a few years. Dispose of them carefully, leaving them to dry out and die for several weeks before composting. It is escapees from gardens that have caused the problems.

I have two new, shiny zinc planters that I'd like to plant up in my front garden. Can I paint them to stop them going weathered and dull?

Shiny zinc? Really? A few years ago I'd have advised you to wipe the surface with a soft cloth covered in oil. I'd have also told you not to splash it with hard tap water, and to repeat the oil treatment a couple of times a year. But those glinting surfaces are a bit 90s-aspirational now, like something a developer would put on the balcony of a luxury apartment. And we all know what happened to them. Let them get weathered and dull: it's the future.

I live on an eco-development with a communal native garden adjacent to dunes in Camber, East Sussex. It was planted with 6m silver birches, which are now dying, and Holm oaks that are now stripped of leaves. What native trees will survive here?

I spoke to Bernard Giffin of English Woodlands Burrow Nursery in East Sussex (ewburrownursery.co.uk), which helps with your council's coastal planting. Those silver birches never stood a chance, not being seaside plants and being too mature to survive those salty winds. But he says to try again with the Holm oaks (not strictly native, but you can't be too picky), this time planting a windbreak of willow or poplar, too. Forget instant impact and start with small plants, expecting only 12.5cm–15cm growth a year. Add lots of organic matter to the sand before planting, and stake well. Hawthorn should also do well. Plant now to mid-March.

The fence at the bottom of my garden is a magnet for kids who climb our trees. What can I plant as a barrier? I know there are prickly hedges, but would prefer something that grows quickly with no planting, such as seeds.

Kids, eh? Why can't they find some innocent, harmless activity? There are lots of very quick-growing annual climbers – such as black-eyed Susan, cup and saucer vine and even sweet peas – that you could start sowing now from seed and which would cover the fence in no time. But these are pretty impotent in the face of determined schoolchildren and they will last just one season. I'm afraid it's a prickly hedge and a little planting for you. To keep the effort to a minimum, choose one that forms a thicket, such as the white-stemmed bramble (Rubus cockburnianus), or one that you can train to cover the whole fence, such as pyracantha. The more plants you use, the sooner you will scotch these menaces to society.

What to do this week

Unless you have been living it up on supermarket basil all winter, the poor old taste buds will be desperate for some fresh herbs by now. Cast aside that old jar of dusty mixed herbs and go out and dig up a few sections of mint: there is always plenty to spare. Pop the roots into pots of compost and stand them on a sunny windowsill indoors. The warmth of the house will bring the mint into growth long before it gets going outdoors.

February to April is a critical period for feeding birds, as berries are running low and insects are not yet out in force. Fat means survival, so think chopped bacon rinds, mild grated cheese and fat cakes made from seeds mixed into melted lard or suet. Mix things up with a bit of chopped apple and some raisins and, ideally, provide quality wild birdseed. Bird baths need unfrozen water – for bathing as well as drinking. All of this will see your local birds fighting fit for the frenzy of breeding just around the corner.

It seems a waste to buy lots of shiny new pots for seedlings when they will only be in use for a month or so. Plastic milk containers do the job just as well. Start stockpiling one-pinters now for the seed-sowing frenzy ahead. Slice off the tops and make several holes in the base for drainage. You will have pots that are light and easy to move around – each having its own little handle – and above all, exceedingly cheap. Recycling without the middleman.

End of February

About 18 months ago, I had a diseased apple tree removed and the ground around it treated for honey fungus. An adjacent privet hedge has since become dead in parts, and the ground beneath sprouted mushrooms. Should I get the whole hedge removed? Can I replace sections, or must it now be a fence?

Honey fungus spreads by feeding off dead wood (perhaps, in your case, remaining roots of the apple tree) and rampaging around the garden, searching out susceptible plants or dead wood to colonise. Privet is particularly susceptible. Replace it with something with more resistance (choose from yew, beech and box). Honey fungus doesn't usually attack anything that is healthy, so give your plants a feed with chicken manure pellets, a good soaking and a mulch to keep in moisture. If you do put up a fence, treat the wood with preservative, use metal bases for the posts and make sure no wood is in contact with the soil, as honey fungus can colonise fences, too.

I've always been a very timid pruner (if at all), but know I should cut back my shrub roses in spring. When, exactly? In March, they're already showing new shoots and I haven't the heart to cut them back, but isn't it bad to do it when there are frosts?

Now is a good time. It's OK to chop off a few new shoots, and a bit of frost is not a problem. Choose a mild day, and check no frost is forecast for that night, because stems can be damaged when just pruned – a spell of really cold weather after pruning could conceivably cause some die back, which looks dark brown and should be cut out. Don't panic, though: the worst possible outcome would be a week or two's delay in flowering. Now here's how to do it: using sharp secateurs (and loppers or a pruning saw for the thick bits), first remove anything dead or damaged, or that looks diseased. Next, take out the thickest and woodiest of the stems.

Then create a bowl shape, with an open middle, by cutting out any growths that emerge from the centre or that cross it – this allows air to circulate freely, so reducing disease problems later. Finally, reduce your remaining stems by about two-thirds, always pruning down to an outward-pointing bud, visualising the continuation of your open bowl shape as the shoots grow. The flush of new growth that'll be stimulated by a stiff pruning will be much more floriferous than the stuff currently clogging up your bushes: you'll wonder why you didn't do it sooner. Be firm, and you'll be rewarded.

A year ago, one of our cats (obese and not inclined to move about much) started defecating in our flowerbed. We netted it to discourage him and gave him a litter tray, but now he goes on the lawn, which is a problem because we have two young children. How can I keep him off the grass?

Unfortunately, your best option seems to be to encourage the cat back into the border. Cats usually choose bare soil to do their business in and if your border is densely planted, a newly created bare patch will be tempting and may keep the poo in a manageable area that can be regularly cleared. At the same time, make it difficult for him to get on to the lawn by stretching string across, held a few inches from the ground by pegs, in a grid system. If there are bare patches on the lawn, these might attract him, so take this opportunity to re-seed it before it gets hit by spring wear and tear from the little ones.

I am considering planting thyme or chamomile between paving slabs. Which varieties are appropriate? Can I sow seed or do I have to buy plants?

There are plenty of low-growing herbs that do well planted between paving. The beauty of this is that just walking around your garden releases wafts of herby oils. You need ones that cope well with being trodden on. Creeping thyme (Thymus serpyllum) and its cultivars almost seem to like it. 'Minimus' is particularly compact and has pink flowers 'Goldstream' has gold variegated leaves and a lemony scent. The best chamomile to use is Chamaemelum nobile 'Treneague', which is a non-flowering type that spreads well. Also consider Corsican mint (Mentha requienii) and creeping savory (Satureja spicigera). You could sow seed of the creeping thyme, mint and savory in a propagator or greenhouse now, or wait until May and sow them directly into the gaps, after roughing up the soil. The camomile and thyme cultivars have to be propagated by cuttings or divisions, as they may not come true from seed. However, their mat-forming habit means they are constantly putting down new roots, so one small plant can go a long way. Buy a couple of plants and split them, making sure each has a good section of leaf and root. Plant out between the cracks, and keep them well watered over the first summer.

My conservatory-grown orange and lemon trees look healthy, but the leaves are covered in little white grubs and small flies. The leaves are sticky. How can I clear the problem?

The stickiness is down to honeydew, a dainty euphemism for the substance that shoots out of the back end of aphids (the flies) and mealy bugs (white grubs). These sap suckers are quietly draining the life from your trees and making them less resistant to other attacks. Repeat applications of insecticidal soap works well on aphids. Buy it from garden centres, or make an extremely dilute washing-up liquid solution in a spray bottle. The coating around mealy bugs repels water, so prise these off individually with cotton buds dipped in methylated spirits. Wash the leaves with a soapy solution. As the plants are in a conservatory, consider biological controls Aphidius and Cryptolaemus (ladybirdplantcare.co.uk).

I've read a lot about the decline of bees and would like to keep some in my garden. How do I go about it? Do I need permission from the neighbours?

You don't need permission, but it is obviously nice to ask, and to do everything you can to prevent the bees from becoming a problem for them. You should avoid siting the hives near paths or areas where the neighbours (or you, for that matter) walk frequently. You can also place the hives facing a barrier to force them to fly up and away, rather than across a path or garden. Netting will do, but a hedge is better. There is a lot to it, and you would do well to join the British Bee Keepers Association. I would also encourage you to look into Warré beekeeping, in which the hive is only opened once a year, with new boxes added underneath, which prevents the loss of heat that may stress the bees. Warré keepers also leave honey in the hives for the bees to overwinter on, rather than feeding them on sugar water, which makes sense to me.

What to do this week

The annual display of bluebells carpeting British woodlands in April and May must be one of the horticultural wonders of the world. Planting them on a smaller scale will just make you appreciate the individual flowers all the more. Each flower spike holds sweetly scented, nodding flowers of iridescent blue. A drift planted under a tree or in a shady corner will bring a hint of late spring woodlands to your garden. Theft of bulbs has decimated some woodlands and it is important to buy bulbs that have been propagated at nurseries. The best way to establish them is to plant them 'in the green', when the bluebells have been lifted with their leaves immediately after flowering.

Get on top of slugs early to avoid seedling carnage. Nemaslug, the slug-sucking nematode, can be applied in the next few weeks, so get your orders in from Green Gardener (greengardener.co.uk) now. In my experience, this early application is the most important, because it keeps the slimy ones at bay just as seedlings and young shoots are at their most tempting. Use copper rings (slugrings.co.uk) to protect individual plants from slugs and snails that escape the cull.

With spring around the corner, it's time to order tender perennials. For something a bit different, go to a specialist. Fir Trees Pelargoniums (firtreespelargoniums.co.uk) is the place for pelargoniums, though I'm also splashing out on cane begonias, some of which have bamboo-like stems, and the bizarre-looking 'parrot plant' impatiens from Dibleys Nurseries (dibleys.com) to give my shady containers a subtropical look. Also whet your appetite with Special Plants' eclectic list (specialplants.net) to enjoy all summer.

Useful links

Plants, seeds and trees

Nurseries

apuldramroses.co.uk

architecturalplants.com - exotics

ashwood-nurseries.co.uk

auriculas.co.uk

avonbulbs.com

beechesnursery.co.uk -
herbaceous specialists

bigplantnursery.co.uk

blackmoor.co.uk - fruit trees

bluebellbulbs.co.uk

blomsbulbs.com

bodwen-nursery.co.uk
- Japanese maples

broadleighbulbs.co.uk

callygardens.co.uk - perennials

cgf.net - perennials

classicroses.co.uk

clifton.co.uk

crug-farm.co.uk - perennials
and woody plants

davidaustinroses.com

dejager.co.uk - bulbs

dibleys.com - house plants

ewburrownursery.co.uk - trees

firtreespelargoniums.co.uk

gee-tee.co.uk - bulbs

graftedwalnuts.co.uk

greatdixter.co.uk

hallsofheddon.co.uk -
chrysanthemum and dahlia specialists

iansturrockandsons.
co.uk - Welsh fruit trees

junker.co.uk - trees and shrubs

keepers-nursery.co.uk - fruit trees

kindergarden.co.uk - hanging
basket and vertical garden plants

larchcottage.co.uk

majesticgroup.co.uk - trees

musgrovewillows.co.uk

national-dahlia-collection.co.uk

pantiles-nurseries.co.uk

phoenixperennials.com

raymondevisonclematis.com

specialplants.net

thorncroftclematis.co.uk

thornhayes-nursery.co.uk
- specialises in broad leaved,
conifer and fruit trees

trevenacross.co.uk - southern
hemisphere plants

turn-it-tropical.co.uk - exotics

victoriananursery.co.uk

Plants

crocus.co.uk

dobies.co.uk

fothergills.co.uk

garden-centre.org

jparkers.co.uk

organiccatalogue.com

organicplants.co.uk

thompson-morgan.com

Seed suppliers

beansandherbs.co.uk

chilternseeds.co.uk

dtbrownseeds.co.uk

herbiseed.com - 'weed'
and wildflower seeds

hdra.org.uk/hsl - heritage seed library

kingsseeds.com

marshalls-seeds.co.uk

nickys-nursery.co.uk

organicseedsonline.com

plantsofdistinction.co.uk

realseeds.co.uk

seaspringseeds.co.uk

seeds-by-size.co.uk

seedsofchange.com

seedsofitaly.com

seedypeople.co.uk - seed swapping

simpsonsseeds.co.uk

suffolkherbs.com

suttons-seeds.co.uk

thomasetty.co.uk

Trees and hedges

allotmentforestry.com

ancienttreehunt.org.uk

forestry.gov.uk

hedgelaying.org.uk

mistle.co.uk

mistletoe.org.uk

treecouncil.org.uk

trees.org.uk - Arboricultural
Association

treeworks.co.uk - Treework
environmental practice

woodland-trust.org.uk

*Gardening
information
and supplies*

Allotments

allotment.info

nagtrust.org - national
allotment gardens trust

Building (patios, paths, raised beds etc)

copperridge.co.uk - for
roof moss issues

diy.com - B&Q

dunweedin.co.uk - rubber
bark and soft, safe surfaces

fieldguard.com - rubber mats

focusdiy.co.uk

gardenorganic.org.uk/
saveourgardens - a plea to go
easy with the building work

kayser-uk.com - railway sleepers

pavingexpert.com

railwaysleeper.com

romseyreclamation.
com - railway sleepers

screwpegs.com - screw in
awning and tent pegs

thechildrensstore.co.uk - for
safety matting etc

ukmediation.net

Compost

amlc.co.uk - manure to your door

bokashibucket.co.uk

compostawarenessweek.org.uk

dalefootcomposts.co.uk - more
manure to your door

General

agralan.co.uk

alexander-rose.co.uk
- garden furniture

alitags.co.uk - plant labels

burgonandball.com - tools

dobbies.co.uk

ferndale-lodge.co.uk

gardena.co.uk

harrodhorticultural.com

just-green.com

keengardener.co.uk

labourandwait.co.uk

originalorganics.co.uk

plantmenow.co.uk

primrose-london.co.uk

sarahraven.com

spanishrings.com - Spanish
wall planters

thegardenersshop.co.uk

thegardenfactory.co.uk

thenaturalgardener.co.uk

wigglywigglers.co.uk

Lawns

easyplants.co.uk - fake grass

evergreensuk.com - more fake grass

rolawndirect.co.uk

torowheelhorse.co.uk - mowers etc

Living roofs and walls

kindergarden.co.uk

livingroofs.org

mclawlivingroofs.co.uk

verticalgardenpatrickblanc.com

Misc

britisheco.com - renewable energy

cat.org.uk - Centre for
Alternative Technology

freecycle.org

greenwarehouse.co.uk - eco store

guerillagardening.org

lunarorganics.com

museumgardenhistory.org

nigelsecostore.co.uk

spot-on-sundials.co.uk

thewellyshop.com

zooceramics.co.uk

National institutions

kew.org

nationaltrust.org.uk

rhs.org.uk

rspb.org.uk

Pest and disease control

blightwatch.co.uk

deteracat.co.uk

greengardener.co.uk

herbal-shop.co.uk - suppliers of neem tree oil

ladybirdplantcare.co.uk

nemasysinfo.com

slugrings.co.uk

ukorganics.co.uk

waspinator.co.uk

Ponds / aquatics

gartenart.co.uk

green-ways.co.uk

henleywatergardens.co.uk

pondsafety.com

Watering

hozelock.com

rainwaterhog.co.uk

waterbuttsdirect.co.uk

Wildlife

bto.org/nnbw - national nest box week

mothcount.brc.ac.uk

Recommended gardens

abbotsbury-tourism.co.uk/gardens.htm
- Abbotsbury Subtropical Gardens, Dorset

botanic.cam.ac.uk - Cambridge Botanic Garden

camboestate.com - Cambo Estate in Fife

cat.org.uk - the Centre for Alternative Technology, Machynlleth, Powys

cottesbrookehall.co.uk - Cottesbrooke Hall in Northampton

eastlambrook.co.uk - East Lambrook in Somerset

gardenofwales.org.uk - National Botanic Garden of Wales, Llanarthny, Camarthen

garden-organic.co.uk - organic display gardens at Ryton, Warwickshire, Audley End, Essex and Yalding, Kent

greatdixter.co.uk - Great Dixter, East Sussex

kew.org - Kew Gardens

nationaltrust.org.uk/main/w-Stourhead - Stourhead, Wiltshire

ngs.org.uk - National gardens scheme, which lists gardens open for charity and publishes The Yellow Book

rbge.org.uk - Royal Botanic Garden Edinburgh

rbge.org.uk/the-gardens/logan - Logan Botanic Garden, exotic plants in an area of Scotland warmed by the Gulf Stream

rhs.org.uk/gardens - details of the four RHS gardens and RHS recommended gardens plus a link to the RHS garden finder

snowdrops.co.uk - Hodsock Priory in Nottinghamshire

Recommended reading

The Royal Horticultural Society's *Plant Finder* is published every year. To the uninitiated, it looks like a dry compilation of Latin names and obscure initials, but once you crack the code (not nearly as hard as I make it sound), you gain access to every obscure plant you can think of, plus hundreds of fabulous, specialist nurseries.

Long to garden but don't have space? *Growing Stuff: An Alternative Guide To Gardening* (Black Dog) is an unusual book that doesn't presume everyone has a patch of their own. The merry band of authors show how the frustrated can channel their enthusiasms by container growing, harvesting wild plants, guerrilla gardening and even horticultural art installations.

My allotment bible is *Grow Your Own Vegetables* (Frances Lincoln), by the marvellous Joy Larkcom – my copy is covered in mud and thoroughly well thumbed. It is a no-nonsense affair, but she has other books (with pretty pictures) on the more creative side of vegetable gardening, such as *Creative Vegetable Gardening* (Mitchell Beazley). In it she argues that practical can also be beautiful – she sees the beds in her potager as 'framed canvases waiting for their paintings', and discusses the most architectural of edibles as well as cut-and-come-again leaf crops, seed heads, living edges and climbing plants for the most dramatic effects.

Pest-control books don't come much more right-on than *The Little Book Of Garden Villains*, by Allan Shepherd. Running through the top 10 pests (top as in most troublesome, not favourite), it urges readers to step away from the chemicals and try barriers, traps, biological controls, good garden health and plant selection. It is a funny, easy read, and is produced by the Centre for Alternative Technology on recycled paper (cat.org.uk).

A good place to discover the intricacies of companion gardening is Bob Flowerdew's *Complete Book Of Companion Gardening* (Kyle Cathie). For a wider perspective, any vegetable book with an organic bent will cover companion planting to some extent. HDRA's *Encyclopedia Of Organic Gardening* (Dorling Kindersley), Andi Clevely's *The Allotment Book* (Collins) and Bob Flowerdew's *Organic Bible* (Kyle Cathie) all do so, and also cover other organic pest-control methods, such as the use of physical protection and biological control. All are pretty handy places to start, as is, dare I say it, my own *The Half-Hour Allotment* (Frances Lincoln).

Vegetable guru Sue Stickland's book, *Back Garden Seed Saving* (Eco-Logic Books/Worldly Goods) offers tips on harvesting and storing your own seeds (most should last about three years if stored well). It also contains introductions to lesser-known varieties and a crop-by-crop guide to saving seed.

From the end of September to mid October it is officially tree seed collecting season. The Tree Council wants us to get out and collect and sow tree seeds, the aim being to build up a stock of trees perfectly adapted to our local climate. This annual fiesta of collecting has been happening since 1999 and a book, *Trees And How To Grow Them*, was published to celebrate its 10th anniversary. It is an illustrated guide to 80 native and ornamental trees and a handy practical guide to growing your own future forest. Go to treecouncil.org. uk for more details.

If you are overwhelmed by the fantastic range of roses that's out there, try Dermot O'Neill's *Roses Revealed* (Kyle Cathie), which is full of enthusiasm and great pictures, but, more importantly, is split into helpful segments entitled Roses For Security, Roses For Shaded Positions, Roses For Balconies And Roof Gardens, and so on. In other words, there's something for every gardener.

Clematis makes a surprisingly good climber for pots and Raymond Evison's *Clematis For Small Spaces* (Timber Press) introduces the reader to 150 of those best suited to patios, decks, balconies and hanging baskets. In it he recommends the new Boulevard Collection, as he would, having bred them, but they do give good value: flowering along the stems, rather than the tips, and producing two, even three flushes of flowers each summer (raymondevisonclematis.com).

Finally, something of a curiosity. *Men And Sheds* (New Holland) by Gordon Thorburn looks at 40 men, their sheds and what they get up to in them, all documented in lovely black-and-white photos. Needless to say, these outbuildings are not all shrines to terracotta pots, compost and the lawnmower.

Index